EASTBOURNE OR BUST

Cycling the South Downs Way

Paul Amess

Kingston House

Contents

Title Page
Eastbourne or Bust: The South Downs Way
Introduction
Getting South — 1
Winchester to Chidden — 5
Chidden to Gumber Bothy — 37
Gumber Bothy to Truleigh — 70
Truleigh to Eastbourne — 96
Conclusion — 150

Eastbourne Or Bust: The South Downs Way

This is a book about cycling the South Downs Way. It's also a book about questionable decision-making, sore limbs, and shouting into the wind while pretending I'm having a lovely time.

I set out thinking it would be scenic, wholesome, and mildly heroic — an epic journey across England's green and pleasant land. What I got was mud, sweat, sunburn, spiritual crises, and a growing suspicion that the people who designed this route were deeply unwell.

Along the way, I met lovely humans, not-so-lovely humans, a suspicious number of dogs who wanted to lick me to death, and hills that felt personally vindictive. There was rain. There was drama. There was a brief moment when I considered faking an injury and calling a taxi. But somehow, I made it from one end to the other, powered by stubbornness, snacks, and the fading hope that the finish line would be something more exciting than a bloody car park.

If you're looking for a helpful guide full of practical tips and inspirational messages, you may want to put this book down immediately. Probably best to burn it. But if you're here for the sarcasm, the swearing, the history lessons you didn't ask for, and the comforting sound of someone else suffering for your entertainment — you're in exactly the right place.

Strap in. It's going to be a very bumpy ride.

Introduction

The South Downs Way
Or: How I Decided to Cycle Across Southern England Like a Masochist with a Death Wish and a Screw Loose (Several, Actually — On the Bike)

Right, let's get this out of the way up front: most people walk the South Downs Way. Sensible, booted-up, flask-wielding types who enjoy a nice picnic on a hill and the gentle sensation of their joints slowly turning to dust. But me? No, I looked at those gentle rolling hills, that endless chalk trail, and thought, "You know what this needs? A rusty old bicycle that changes gear when it feels like it — usually backwards — and a rider who hasn't done a squat since P.E. in 1998."

Because apparently I hate myself.

The South Downs Way is 100 miles of rugged National Trail stretching from the genteel cobbles of Winchester, all medieval charm and people pretending not to be posh, to Eastbourne — a seaside town best described as a retirement brochure that got left out in the rain. It was first waymarked in 1972, a year famous for flared trousers, brown décor, and terrible decisions. Fitting, really. But the route itself? Oh, it's been around a while. We're talking Bronze Age. Before satnavs. Before roads. Before bikes. A time when people wandered up these chalky ridges in animal skins, possibly because they'd misplaced their woolly mammoth and needed a better view.

And what did they see? Well, what *you'll* see, assuming your eyeballs aren't vibrating out of your skull from the constant rattling, is some of the most ludicrously scenic countryside in Britain. Rolling hills. Endless skies. Far-off church spires. Sheep. So many sheep. Silent, judging, unmoved by your suffering. You'll pass Iron Age hillforts (basically prehistoric cul-de-sacs), Norman churches that look like they were dropped there by a bored god, and views over the Weald that are so picturesque they ought to come with a warning: "May induce smugness."

And let's talk terrain. Oh, the terrain. The South Downs Way is made almost entirely of chalk — a substance that has all the grip of a buttered eel and turns into a slip-and-slide of doom the moment it rains. Which it will. Frequently. And if it's not raining, it's bone-dry and rutted like someone's tried to recreate the surface of the moon using only bike tyres and bitterness. Your arms will buzz. Your teeth will chatter. Your bike will develop new and exciting sounds, most of them in minor keys.

But still, I chose this. I *chose* to drag my two-wheeled scrapyard over every sodding undulation of this ancient escarpment like some sort of lycra-clad Sisyphus. Why? Because I wanted the views. The solitude. The sense of achievement. And also because I naively believed "cycling" meant "easier than walking."

Spoiler: it doesn't.

So buckle up (figuratively — there are no seatbelts on bikes, more's the pity), lower your expectations, and prepare to question every life decision that's led you to this moment. The South Downs Way awaits — 100 miles of thigh-burning, brake-squealing, scenery-soaked glory. And me? I'm doing it on a bike that's held together with cable ties, hope, and the occasional expletive.

Let's ride. (And push. And swear. And ride again.)

Getting South

No great adventure begins without a pilgrimage, and mine started in the frozen North — Yorkshire — where the sun is a rumour and people wear shorts in a blizzard "because it's not that bad." I boarded my train south like a modern-day explorer, full of hope, snacks, and deeply misplaced confidence in the British railway system.

That confidence lasted all of eight minutes.

First, the train was cancelled. Not delayed. *Cancelled.* Like a disgraced 90s pop star. No explanation, just a cheery "sorry for the inconvenience" from the tannoy, like that somehow covers the fact that my carefully timed connection was now as useful as a chocolate tyre lever. After some Olympic-level platform hopping and a full-body sprint that nearly sent me into cardiac arrest in front of a Pumpkin Café, I caught a replacement train with a window the size of a letterbox and the ambient temperature of Satan's greenhouse.

And that's when *she* happened.

I had a reserved seat. *Reserved.* With my name digitally stamped on it like destiny. But when I got there, some woman had not only parked herself in it like a throne but had spread out her bags like she was planning to sublet. When I gently mentioned the small matter of the reservation, she looked up with the faux innocence of someone who's just claimed squatters' rights and said, "Oh, are *you* 45B?"

No. I'm Beyoncé. Move.

Eventually, I found a seat in a carriage that smelled faintly of crisps and existential despair, and I passed the rest of the journey clutching my bike, my patience, and a rising suspicion that this trip was already trying to kill me.

And I hadn't even started pedalling yet.

I arrived in Winchester on a glorious summer's evening, the sort that tricks you into thinking England is a pleasant place. Birds were chirping, the sun was doing that golden-hour Instagram nonsense, and the entire city looked like it had been airbrushed by a tourist board with something to prove. It was all very tranquil — right up until I got off the train, pointed Google Maps in the general direction of my B&B, and immediately got *completely and utterly lost*.

Winchester, as it turns out, is not a city. It's a medieval riddle with a postcode. Streets wind around in nonsensical loops, alleyways disappear into thin air, and every building looks like it could be either a museum or a really pretentious bakery. At one point, I walked past the same cathedral three times from three different angles, like it was following *me*.

And the cathedral? Oh, it's huge. Stonkingly huge. Once the longest in Europe, because apparently Winchester had a mild case of cathedral envy. Inside, it holds the bones of ancient kings, medieval saints, and, in a surprise literary twist, Jane Austen — because nothing says "pride and prejudice" like being buried next to a bishop.

Finally, after several laps of the same cobbled square, I located my B&B, tucked away behind a hedge that looked sentient. The door creaked open to reveal the proprietor: a small, hunched man who spoke exclusively in cryptic aphorisms, like he'd fallen out of a fortune cookie and never recovered.

"You seek rest, yes," he said, eyes twinkling like he knew how I was going to die. "Upstairs your destiny lies, but mind the second step — it is a liar."

Sorry, what?

He handed me a key on a fob the size of

a grapefruit and disappeared into the shadows, possibly to consult a cauldron or whisper riddles to a moth. I hauled my bike up two flights of stairs that actively tried to kill me and flopped onto the world's squeakiest bed, wondering if I'd accidentally booked a room in an Arthurian side quest.

But hey — the sheets were clean, the kettle worked, and I hadn't been turned into a frog. So, on balance? A strong start.

Winchester To Chidden

Day 1. Everything Hurts and the Bike is Haunted.

I woke up in Winchester to the soothing sounds of traffic, birdsong, and someone outside arguing passionately about sourdough. The sun was shining, my legs hadn't yet realised what I was about to do to them, and it was time for breakfast.

Downstairs, my host — still every inch the budget Yoda — greeted me with a solemn nod and the cryptic phrase: "Eat well, you must — for the path ahead is long. The toast — it has moods."

Right. Cool.

The breakfast was… unusual. A sort of DIY affair involving three different types of jam (all labelled *"experimental"*), some home-smoked mackerel that looked like it had survived a small fire, and porridge that may or may not have been sentient. He served it all while muttering things like "The cereal knows your fears" and "Do not provoke the marmalade." I nodded politely, avoided eye contact with the marmalade, and ate everything quickly in case it ate *me* first.

Fed, slightly traumatised, and fully caffeinated, I wheeled my noble steed — aka the bike that screams in protest every time I change gear — out into the warm morning air. Time for a quick sightseeing loop before officially starting the trail, because what better way to prepare for a hundred-mile ride than by pointlessly riding in circles first?

Winchester, it turns out, is absolutely stuffed with history. Proper history. The kind that involves swords, saints, and people called things like Æthelflæd. It was once the capital of England back when England was still figuring out how vowels worked. King Alfred the Great ruled from here — a man so historically important they stuck a statue of him in the middle of town holding a sword the size of a canoe and looking like he's about to smite the next person who complains about the parking.

I bumped and rattled my way down ancient, cobbled streets that felt specifically designed to dismantle a bicycle bolt by bolt. By the time I'd passed the Great Hall — with its legendary Round Table that *definitely* wasn't just a massive dinner tray — and looped around Winchester College (posh, old, smells of Latin and ambition), my bike was already making noises like a tortured xylophone.

Every stone, every wobble, every medieval manhole cover was a personal attack. By the time I reached the outskirts of town, I was pretty sure I'd left a trail of nuts, washers, and probably one pedal behind me. A local jogger gave me a look that said, *"Is that thing legal?"* and frankly, I wasn't sure either.

But I was off. The South Downs Way had officially begun. The sun was out, the road ahead was calling, and if my bike could just hold itself together with sheer spite and leftover marmalade vibes from breakfast, then maybe — just maybe — I had a chance.

Before I even set rubber to chalk, I'd done my homework. Or, more accurately, I'd fallen down a terrifying rabbit hole of South Downs Way advice pages that made the whole thing sound less like a bike ride and more like a survival reality show with slightly better scenery.

According to the so-called "experts," tackling this trail requires not just fitness, determination, and a questionable grasp of geography, but also a full emergency kit. I was advised — quite seriously — to bring a repair kit, a first aid kit, a backup first aid kit in case the first one spontaneously combusts, two litres of water *at all times*, snacks for at least three apocalypses, a personal locator beacon, and, I kid you not, *an emergency bivvy bag.*

In case I —what? — get overtaken by fog and have to bivouac next to a startled sheep?

Apparently, phone signal is "patchy," the route is "remote," and the terrain is "challenging" — which is English for "your bike will cry, your thighs will file for divorce, and at least once you'll hallucinate a pub that isn't there."

The path is also shared with walkers, horses, and rogue sheep who, I was warned, "can be territorial." I'm sorry, *territorial sheep*? Are they going to challenge me to a duel? Will I be mugged by a ewe with attitude and a switchblade?

There are also stern warnings about "exposure on the ridges," which I assume means "there is weather here sometimes all of it at once." Wind that'll blow your helmet clean off, rain that feels like being pelted with gravel, and sun so strong you'll roast like a hog on a spit *unless* you reapply SPF 50 every four seconds like a vampire on a beach holiday.

All this, and I haven't even *started* pedalling yet.

Still, I took it all seriously. I packed tools I don't know how to use, snacks I will absolutely eat out of boredom before the first hill, and a poncho that makes me look like a sweaty tent. What could possibly go wrong?

Let's find out.

With Winchester's ancient charm fading behind me, I ventured eastward, following the River Itchen's serene path. This gentle introduction to the South Downs Way was soon interrupted by a stark reminder of modernity: the M3 motorway.

Crossing the M3 via a footbridge felt like stepping from a Jane Austen novel into a scene from a dystopian film. The roar of traffic below contrasted sharply with the tranquility I'd just left. It was as if the trail wanted to test my commitment right from the start.

Beyond the motorway, the path transformed into a rutted track skirting the edge of a vast field. This segment, leading towards the hamlet of Chilcomb, was a true initiation. The uneven terrain challenged my bike's suspension and my resolve. Each bump and groove seemed strategically placed to test the mettle of both rider and machine.

Chilcomb itself emerged as a picturesque cluster of cottages and an ancient church, offering a brief respite and a glimpse into England's pastoral beauty. The journey from Winchester to this point, though short, encapsulated the contrasts of the South Downs Way: historical serenity juxtaposed with modern challenges.

As I pressed on, the trail promised more such

juxtapositions, weaving through landscapes that have witnessed centuries of history, all while demanding the utmost from those who dare to traverse it.

Leaving the charming hamlet of Chilcomb behind, I ventured into a small woodland, where the canopy of beech trees provided a serene tunnel of dappled light. Birdsong filled the air, creating a symphony that accompanied my every pedal stroke. However, the tranquility was momentarily disrupted by a rabbit with a noticeable swagger, who darted across the path, casting a glance that seemed to challenge my presence in his domain.

Emerging from the woods, the path turned rudely skyward in that special South Downs Way way that says, "Hope you weren't too attached to your thighs." Up and up it went, dragging me towards the legendary Cheesefoot Head — a name that sounds less like a scenic viewpoint and more like a foot fungus you catch on a lads' holiday in Magaluf. But I digress.

At the top, the land suddenly dropped into a vast natural amphitheatre, which is the official term for "giant grassy dip." It's genuinely impressive — big skies, sweeping views, and sheep loitering around like they've just finished a philosophy degree and are now pondering existential dread. But the real kicker? This isn't just any scenic dip. This is *Cheesefoot Head*, and it played a starring role in actual world history.

Back in 1944, this grassy bowl became the unlikely stage for one of the most important pep talks of all time. General Dwight D. Eisenhower, Supreme Commander of the Allied Forces and owner of a jawline that could cut granite, stood here and addressed thousands of American troops just before D-Day. He gave them *the* speech — the big one. The "history will remember you" kind of speech. Imagine it: ranks of young soldiers in uniform, the air thick with tension, the knowledge of what lay ahead weighing heavy on every heart. And in the middle of it all, Eisenhower, calm and resolute, rallying them like some sort of military Gandalf with an accent from Kansas.

And now? Now I'm stood in the same spot, Lycra bunched in all the wrong places, trying to fish a half-melted cereal bar out of my saddlebag without dropping my phone down a rabbit hole. The most dangerous operation I'm facing is whether to risk eating it with glovey hands or wipe them on my shorts first.

It's honestly surreal. You expect ghosts, echoes of courage, something deeply profound… and instead, you get a slightly damp backside and a view that makes your knees wobble — but for entirely different reasons than those brave lads in 1944. History is weird like that. One minute, it's a battlefield of bravery. The next, it's you wondering whether that sheep over there is judging your snack choices and quietly wondering how someone with your calves made it this far.

So I sat there for a minute, soaking in the echoes of destiny and heroism, while sweating profusely and eating something that claimed to be apricot-flavoured but tasted like compressed mulch. Eisenhower had the weight of the free world on his shoulders. I had an energy drink leaking in my bag. Close enough.

Heading north from Cheesefoot Head, the trail lulled me into a false sense of countryside serenity — rolling fields, birdsong, that sort of bucolic nonsense — and then, just past Temple Valley, I took a right turn and promptly thought I was hallucinating from overexertion and oat bar fumes. Because there, in a perfectly normal-looking field, was a *tank*. An actual, rumbling, mud-spraying *tank*. Just trundling about like this was the opening scene of Apocalypse Now: Hampshire Edition.

At first, I assumed I'd finally cracked. Maybe the chalk dust had gone to my brain. Maybe I was having a heatstroke vision of the Normandy landings but with more cow parsley. But no — this was real. Welcome to Juniper Leisure: the only place I've ever seen where you can exchange legal tender to drive a vehicle designed for flattening enemy infrastructure. Because apparently quad biking just wasn't aggressive enough for some people.

And look, I get it — everyone needs a hobby. Some knit. Some do yoga. Some pay £300 to roll over a car in a 1960s Chieftain tank while giggling like a Bond villain on his day off. Fair play. Personally, I find it hard enough just keeping my *bike* on the path without going full demolition derby, but sure — pop a helmet on, crush a Renault Clio, call it "therapy." This is Britain. We cope how we must.

Leaving behind the absurd joy of watching a stranger drive a tank across a Hampshire field like they were late for war, the South Downs Way tucked me neatly into a chalky little corridor of trail, hemmed in by trees on either side like nature's own bike lane — if bike lanes were full of roots, ruts, and the lingering smell of compost.

It was shady, peaceful, and gave me just enough time to start thinking, "Hey, maybe this won't be so bad." Which is, of course, when the path opened out and reminded me who was boss. The trees fell away, the trail widened, and suddenly — *boom* — views. Proper ones. Sweeping vistas across the Hampshire countryside, stretching north towards the rolling expanse of the Itchen Valley and the distant folds of the North Wessex Downs, all laid out like a green duvet someone forgot to iron.

It was genuinely beautiful, the kind of view that

makes you stop and forget that your water bottle tastes like warm regret. But just as I was soaking it all in, I met a truly British menace: the pothole. My first of the journey. A crater of such malevolent depth it probably had its own climate system. I swerved around it with the grace of a man dodging a wasp in flipflops and very nearly launched myself into the undergrowth.

Welcome to the South Downs Way, where ancient beauty coexists peacefully with crumbling infrastructure.

Moments later, the path spat me out unceremoniously onto a proper main road — Redfield Lane — reminding me, once again, that no matter how deep into the countryside you go, you're never more than five minutes from a Vauxhall Astra doing 60 in a 40 and a dead badger in varying states of ambiguity.

I crossed quickly, praying my bike didn't choose that moment to shed a wheel, and rolled on toward whatever delight awaited next — hopefully something involving fewer near-death experiences and marginally more snacks.

Leaving behind the joys of Redfield Lane — a stretch of tarmac so aggressively ordinary it could have been designed by a focus group on beige — I bounced my way back onto the South Downs Way proper, which had thankfully remembered it was supposed to be scenic again. The path opened up into wide, glorious countryside, all big skies and sweeping fields, with just enough breeze to cool my face and carry the distant sounds of tractors and sheep-related negotiations.

It was one of those stretches where you feel on top of the world — until you hit a patch of loose chalk and your back wheel tries to overtake your front. Still, I carried on, triumphant if slightly dusty, and eventually the path curved south again, narrowing into a beautiful green tunnel of trees. The canopy closed overhead like some sort of enchanted woodland portal, which would have felt magical if I hadn't already inhaled half a hedge and started wondering if that weird nettle sting on my leg was developing sentience.

And that's when we met *them*.

A couple, striding confidently towards us in matching activewear so brightly coloured they could have been seen from space. He had the manic energy of a man who'd eaten three protein bars too many, and she had a walking pole in each hand like she was expecting to be ambushed by goblins at any moment.

"Bit warm for cycling, isn't it?" he chirped, in that helpful way people do when they're not the ones slowly marinating in their own lycra.

"Oh, we don't follow the trail," she added, gesturing vaguely at a bush. "We like to *interpret* it."

Brilliant. We'd found the South Downs Way's first performance artists. I smiled politely, resisted the urge to ask if their map was also interpretive, and pedalled on before I got trapped in a conversation about chakras or artisan granola.

The trail narrowed even more, the trees whispering ominously, and I started wondering if I'd actually passed through some sort of enchanted wardrobe and was now cycling towards Narnia. Either way, it was clear: weirdness levels were rising. And I hadn't even crossed the A272 yet.

Crossing the A272 felt like escaping a motorway-themed video game and landing straight back into a postcard — rolling fields, sun-drenched meadows, and that unmistakable crunch of chalk under tyres that says, "Your bum's not going to thank you for this tomorrow." The terrain heading south was classic South Downs: beautiful, bumpy, and determined to shake your fillings loose. The path undulated like a polite rollercoaster, just hilly enough to make you question your lunch choices but not so bad you'd start drafting a will.

And then, like a mirage shimmering in the heat haze, there it was: *The Milbury's* at Beauworth. Glorious, rustic, mildly overpriced — basically everything you want in a countryside pub when your legs are staging a protest. The pub garden was heaving, full of people wearing expressions that said "We are *definitely* outdoorsy," while clutching pints like they'd just invented beer. I managed to snag one of the last picnic benches, wedged between a hedge and a woman whose sunhat could've doubled as a carport. I ordered some artisan sandwich nonsense that cost more than my rear bike light and came with three crisps and a vague hint of coleslaw. And I got sunburnt for free. Lovely.

But the true entertainment came in the form of *Nigel*, a man in full tweed — waistcoat, trousers, the works — who had clearly mistaken the pub garden for an audition for "Countryfile: The Musical." He was sipping scalding hot tea in 27-degree heat like some kind of sweat-powered locomotive and regaling the surrounding tables with a tale so absurd I almost choked on my artisan chutney.

It was, he explained, "the badger incident."

Apparently, a rogue badger had taken up residence in his garden and "wouldn't leave the begonias alone." What followed was a full-blown stand-off that involved a cricket bat, a foghorn, and, by his account, "a firm but respectful discussion about boundaries." He even mimed the standoff, arms outstretched, as if reenacting the final scene from a David Attenborough documentary directed by Quentin Tarantino.

Honestly, it was better than lunch. I mean, I came for a pub stop and ended up getting live theatre *and* a lecture on badger diplomacy. The South Downs Way was already proving itself to be equal parts stunning, ridiculous, and completely unhinged.

Perfect.

After leaving the oasis of Milbury's — fed, watered, and very slightly crispier than when I arrived — I rejoined the route, which, for reasons unclear to anyone with common sense, now decided to throw me onto an actual road. You know, with *cars*. For half a mile or so I pedalled along tarmac while trying to look confident, visible, and not like a startled woodland creature on wheels.

It was all going fine until a driver in a hatchback the colour of an anxiety attack came flying past me with all the grace and caution of a caffeinated wasp in a blender. They gave me about four molecules of space, blasted their horn, and zoomed off like they'd just received news their air fryer was on fire. I swerved, wobbled, and performed a kind of interpretive dance with my handlebars that should've earned me points for artistic impression and bravery in the face of bonnet-based death.

For a brief, glorious moment, I saw my life

flash before my eyes — mostly made up of bike punctures, bad decisions, and the ham sandwich I'd left uneaten at lunch. It was terrifying and also somehow very British: polite rage, undercooked panic, and the strong urge to apologise to the driver for being in *their* way while *not dying*.

Eventually, the road mellowed and I turned off at a place charmingly called *Wind Farm* — which, to be clear, is a regular old farm, not some majestic landscape of renewable energy. No turbines, no spinning blades, just a gate, a slightly suspicious-looking tractor, and a very judgemental collie who watched me like I owed it money.

Still, it was a welcome return to the trail, where the biggest hazards were likely to be ruts, rogue brambles, or getting side-eyed by a cow — not high-velocity hatchbacks and existential dread. Heart still thudding from my brush with vehicular manslaughter, I reminded myself that I'm far better suited to quiet, muddy peril involving passive-aggressive rabbits than dodging two-tonne metal wombats piloted by people who think the speed limit is more of a dare than a rule.

I should probably mention the ancient, ongoing war between motorists and cyclists at this point — a rivalry as old as time, or at least as old as Lycra. It's a tale of mutual misunderstanding, passive-aggressive gestures, and shared British roads that feel just wide enough for one fragile ego at a time.

See, as a cyclist, I apparently exist solely to irritate drivers. I block their God-given right to shave three seconds off their commute. I have the audacity to be slower, squishier, and more brightly dressed than they'd like. And I ride near the white line and *sometimes even signal*, which is clearly an act of violence.

Motorists, on the other hand, often behave like they're in a Fast & Furious remake — *Surrey Drift* — where the main objective is to overtake anything that moves, preferably while swearing at it through a cracked window and throwing a lukewarm Costa cup out the side.

I try to be the reasonable one. I really do. I use hand signals. I wear high-vis that makes me look like a radioactive traffic cone. I thank them when they don't murder me. But even so, every ride seems to include at least one brush with a driver who thinks cyclists should be relocated to a distant island and only allowed to pedal in circles under strict supervision.

And let's be honest: I'm not exactly helping our cause. I look like a startled chicken on wheels. My bike creaks like it's haunted. My cornering is less "Tour de France" and more "shopping trolley with a loose wheel." So when I wobble into view, I imagine drivers feel the same dread as when you see someone carrying a ladder across a busy road.

All this means that unfortunately, this definitely won't be the last near-death encounter on this trip. Even as I speak, somewhere out there is another motorist revving up their Fiat 500 and squinting suspiciously at anything with handlebars. And I'll be there, squeaking up a hill at 6mph, wearing enough fluorescent fabric to signal aircraft, quietly hoping we can all just get along.

Or, failing that, at least not end up on a dashcam compilation on YouTube.

So, it was with genuine relief — and borderline glee — that I found myself back on a good old-fashioned chalk track. Sure, it rattled my bones like a cheap maraca and coated everything I owned in a fine dust that now lived in my pores, but at least it wasn't trying to *kill me with mirrors and impatience*. Give me uneven terrain, stinging nettles and the constant threat of a rogue pheasant over homicidal hatchbacks any day.

Not far along, I spotted a lone hiker who'd set up what could only be described as a full-blown picnic operation. Blanket, Thermos, a slab of cheese the size of a paving stone — he was living the countryside dream. As I clanked to a stop and tried to discreetly shake the feeling back into my wrists, he looked up, nodded like a man who'd seen things, and said, "Hard work, isn't it? I walked from Winchester this morning. My legs are mostly theoretical now."

I replied, "I've cycled it. My arse is filing a formal complaint and requesting new management."

He offered me a grape and said, "You lot are brave, I'll give you that. Or daft. It's a fine line."

I declined the grape (it looked like it had been handled by a raccoon) and we both turned to admire the view, which was genuinely spectacular — rolling hills, golden fields, and the distant shimmer of something that might have been the sea or was maybe just wishful thinking.

"Beautiful, isn't it?" he said.

"Absolutely," I replied. "Makes you almost forget you're slowly disintegrating from the waist down."

He raised his Thermos like a toast, and I rattled off down the trail, oddly buoyed by the camaraderie of shared suffering and cheese.

Just past Lomer Farm — where the path momentarily flattens out and your legs stop whispering threats — I crossed paths with another trail: the *Wayfarer's Walk*. I know, I know. You think you're doing one walk and then another one just *shows up*, uninvited, like a distant relative who's heard you've got snacks.

So what is the Wayfarer's Walk? Well, it's a 71-mile long-distance path that stretches from Walbury Hill in Berkshire — the highest point in southeast England and a great place to be blown sideways into a hedge — all the way to Emsworth on the Hampshire coast, where walkers presumably finish their journey, remove their boots, and stare into the sea wondering what the hell just happened.

It's named the *Wayfarer's Walk*, which sounds poetic and noble, conjuring up images of cloaked travellers wandering misty hills dispensing wisdom and oatcakes. In reality, it's mostly a collection of farm tracks, bridleways, and moments of confusion where you're not entirely sure if you're still on the trail or have accidentally entered a livestock-based labyrinth.

The route passes through some lovely — and occasionally bonkers — bits of countryside: rolling downland, chalky ridges, ancient woodlands, and more villages with names like someone spilled Scrabble tiles (think: Cheriton, Hambledon, and Abbotstone). It often shares sections with other trails, like the South Downs Way and the Clarendon Way, because these paths are all clearly in a complicated, open relationship.

But there it was, suddenly intersecting with our route like a hiker's version of a motorway slip road, quietly judging me for my Lycra and suspicious energy gels. I nodded respectfully in its direction — trail etiquette and all that — before continuing on my way, safe in the knowledge that the only Wayfaring I was doing today involved increasingly squeaky bicycle saddles and a strong desire for snacks.

Just after Lomer Farm, if you squint hard and use a bit of imagination (and possibly a time machine), you'll stumble across the ghostly remains of *Lomer*, a once-bustling medieval village that has since taken early retirement from existence.

Back in the day, Lomer was a thriving little place. Then, along came the Black Death, and — shockingly — that didn't do wonders for the population. Those who weren't wiped out by plague were probably finished off by the cheery joys of *enclosure*, a lovely historical moment when wealthy landowners decided communal farming was a bit too 14th-century and promptly booted everyone off the land. Charming.

Now, all that remains of Lomer is a collection of grassy humps, dips, and the vague suggestion of "something definitely used to be here." You won't find a Starbucks, a souvenir shop, or even a sign saying "Welcome to Lomer, Please Die Historically." Just a few lumps in a field and the ghost of a medieval peasant shouting, "This was all houses once!"

It's now a *Scheduled Monument*, which basically means English Heritage has officially declared, "Yes, this is where things went horribly wrong, and no, we don't plan to fix it." But if you stop for a moment, you can almost picture the little church, the cottages, the pigs wandering around like they owned the place... and then the slow, inevitable realisation that cholera, death taxes, and rich people with fences were coming.

So if you're into historical tragedies with a scenic view, Lomer's your place. Blink and you'll miss it. Actually, blink and you've already missed it. Keep pedalling.

After leaving the medieval ghost village of Lomer behind (and successfully avoiding being possessed by the spirit of a dysentery-riddled turnip farmer), the trail carried on gently for about a mile. It was the kind of riding that lulls you into thinking, "Yes, I *am* quite good at this," just before you hit a patch of flint and remember your thighs are held together with porridge and poor decisions.

Eventually, I rolled into a small car park that looked like half of Hampshire had decided to gather for a casual meet-up of the "SUVs and Sandwiches Appreciation Society." There were cars, children flinging gravel like it was currency, people unfolding OS maps with the seriousness of NATO commanders, and — glory of glories — a *portable toilet*.

And not just any portable toilet. No, no. This was *the* toilet. The Chosen One. The blue box of salvation. Because just as I arrived, a very particular urge began knocking on the door of my dignity with increasing aggression. You know the one. The *"you've-had-too-much-coffee-and-a-slightly-questionable-lunch-situation"* kind of urgency.

I approached the toilet like a medieval pilgrim arriving at a holy shrine. It wasn't glamorous. It wasn't fragrant. But it was *there*. And that was enough.

Relieved and spiritually realigned, I seized the opportunity to make use of the other miracle in my life: my little camping stove. I perched myself on a bench near the edge of the Beacon Hill Nature Reserve — which is absolutely lovely, by the way, and presumably named after the number of people who light signal fires when they see cyclists approaching in Lycra — and brewed up a piping hot coffee.

Nothing screams "man of the outdoors" quite like a slightly wobbly espresso brewed next to a Portaloo while a spaniel tries to steal your oat bar. It was, in its own chaotic way, perfect.

Beacon Hill: come for the nature, stay for the loo.

Alas, all good things must come to an end — especially when they involve hot coffee, a sit-down, and not being on a hill. It was time to press on, tearfully bidding farewell to the Portaloo of Dreams and the vaguely warm bench that had briefly become my emotional support furniture.

Naturally, the trail immediately turned uphill, because of *course* it did. The sort of incline that starts off deceptively gentle before gradually morphing into something that makes your calves file a formal complaint. I gave it a valiant effort, wheezing and pedalling like a broken accordion, but eventually admitted defeat and dismounted, pushing my bike up like a medieval squire escorting a wounded warhorse.

But the view — *the view*. As I trudged upwards, sweaty and slightly offended, the landscape began to open up behind me. Rolling fields stretched into the distance, patchworked in every shade of green, with far-off villages that looked like they'd been placed there by a whimsical god with a fondness for chocolate boxes. It was enough to make you forget, briefly, that your lungs were trying to exit via your ears.

I skirted through the edge of Exton trying to look like I belonged — like I was just a local popping out for a quick spin, not a sunburnt gremlin on a bike that sounded like it was powered by cutlery. The village was so pristine it felt like I'd accidentally cycled into a National Trust gift shop. Neatly trimmed hedges, postcard cottages, and that faint whiff of money and sourdough. Even the stone wall was smug about how straight it was.

Probably has a cleaner.

A quick nod to the church — ancient, lovely, undoubtedly hiding a crypt full of forgotten nobility — and I carried on, completely unbothered by the fact that absolutely no one was around. Presumably the residents were all indoors, sipping something infused with elderflower and judging me silently from behind linen blinds.

Then, just like that, I slipped into Meonstoke. It's basically Exton's equally attractive twin, if twins could also be smug about their historical significance and had a competition for "Most Perfectly Trimmed Lawn." This place has been on the go since before the Romans unpacked their sandals, and it shows — Roman remains, Saxon settlers, probably a cursed well or two — *proper* history. And, in case that wasn't enough to boost its ego, it's also the hometown of Frank Turner. For those unfamiliar, he's a folk-punk singer-songwriter known for heartfelt lyrics, energetic gigs, and giving middle-aged knees everywhere a reason to mosh gently. He's basically what happens when you mix poetry, power chords, and just enough angst to make it radio-friendly. Not that he was busking on the village green or offering passing cyclists a live rendition of *Recovery*, but still — a solid claim to fame for a place that probably doesn't even have a Costa.

I didn't stop long — just enough to admire

another church, another overly competent wall, and question if I should've worn something that didn't make me look like an exhausted banana. Then I rolled on, leaving the picture-perfect past behind, legs aching, gears groaning, and vaguely certain I'd just cycled through a heritage brochure.

Leaving the quiet charm of Meonstoke behind, I rejoined the chalky track with all the enthusiasm of a man who's just remembered he still has to climb a literal hill with a bike that sounds like it's held together by duct tape, spite, and the occasional prayer. It was late in the day, my legs were somewhere between spaghetti and total system collapse, and the air had taken on that golden, cinematic glow that says, "You're about to suffer, but it's going to look *stunning*."

The incline began gently — just enough to lull you into thinking, *"maybe this won't be too bad"* — before revealing its true nature as a long, slow, grinding ascent designed to break spirits and derail chains. The path was a cocktail of chalk, flint, and ankle-twisting ruts, which, for someone pushing an ageing bike and an ageing body, felt personally offensive.

And where was I dragging myself? *Old Winchester Hill*. A place steeped in millennia of history and, apparently, quite a lot of vertical elevation. The summit is home to an Iron Age hillfort dating back to somewhere between 600 and 300 BC — when, presumably, people didn't have the luxury of giving up halfway and going home to watch telly. Oh, and before that? Bronze Age burial barrows. Because nothing says "history" like stacking up sacred burial mounds.

But here's the best bit — during World War II, someone decided this *ancient, archaeologically significant site* would be *perfect* for testing mortars. Yes. Mortars. On an Iron Age hillfort. Because if there's one thing the British are consistently good at, it's respectfully preserving our national heritage by lobbing high explosives at it. I can only imagine the conversation went something like:
"Is this a sacred site of immense historical importance?"
"Yes."
"Brilliant. Let's blow stuff up on it."

Still, once I finally crawled my way to the top, wheezing like a Victorian orphan with consumption, the view was, annoyingly, worth it. Rolling hills stretched off in every direction, the sky turned into an oil painting, and for a brief moment, I forgot that my thighs were now vibrating with rage and regret.

Thankfully — *mercifully* — the South Downs Way spared me the final indignity of actually having to *go over* Old Winchester Hill. Instead, the path sensibly skirts around it, as if the trail itself looked at my sweat-soaked face and thought,

"Yeah, let's not push him over the edge. Literally."

With lungs partially intact and dignity just about hanging on, I followed the path as it curved around the hill to the north, alongside a stretch of woodland that was lovely and shady and full of noises that made me question whether woodland creatures were plotting something. It was here, mid-huff, that I paused for a breather and a squint at the map to see how far I had left to go. The answer? Far enough to make me mutter something unprintable under my breath.

Tonight's destination was somewhere intriguingly called *The Sustainability Centre*, which conjured up images of composting toilets, barefoot flute music, and someone called Moonbeam gently encouraging me to reconnect with the soil. Which, after a day of riding through sun, chalk dust, and the occasional near-death car encounter, honestly sounded fine. If someone wanted to talk to me about recycling while handing me herbal tea and a solar-powered foot massage, I was in.

Besides, if anyone was going to save the planet, it certainly wasn't going to be me — unless the solution to climate change involved being very sweaty in the countryside and swearing at sheep.

The next stretch of riding took me onto what can only be described as England's narrowest road. Honestly, I've seen wider garden paths. It was the kind of road where if you passed another cyclist, you'd have to engage in a polite duel to the death to decide who got to stay upright. But oddly, the motorists here seemed to have manners — actual *manners*. They slowed down, gave me space, and one even smiled, like I wasn't just an inconvenient obstacle between them and their artisanal cider. It was deeply unsettling. I half-wondered if I'd accidentally pedalled into an alternate dimension where drivers respected cyclists and oat milk was the law.

After that brief flirtation with civilisation, I was back on farm tracks — this time made of concrete, which sounds promising until you realise it's cracked, tilted at all the wrong angles, and possibly designed as a training course for rally cars. Still, progress was being made. The sun was dipping behind me, casting that golden glow that makes everything look mildly divine, even if you're wheezing and covered in a fine film of sweat, dust, and despair.

Just as I rolled triumphantly into Whitewool Farm, basking in the smug satisfaction of surviving Old Winchester Hill without needing an air ambulance, I was immediately brought to a halt by a scene that can only be described as *bovine Armageddon*. The farmer — looking like he'd stepped straight out of a 1970s agricultural porn calendar — was herding what must have been *every cow in Hampshire* across the track. Not ten. Not fifty. I'm talking hundreds. A mooing, lumbering tsunami of udders and flatulence, thundering past like they were late for a vegan protest. The stench was apocalyptic. Every single one of them was enthusiastically redecorating the track with a Jackson Pollock of cow shit — some of it still warm, all of it aggressively squelchy. I stood politely, trying not to breathe or cry, while they shuffled by with their giant dead eyes and zero sense of personal space. One particularly judgemental heifer even paused to moo in my face like I'd offended her entire lineage. Once the stampede subsided, I got back on the bike and pedalled straight through the carnage — tyres slipping, dignity dying — as a wave of bovine excrement baptised me into a new and unwelcome phase of the journey: the *shit-covered cyclist*.

The other animals, the wild ones, were starting to emerge for their nightly shift — rabbits darting across the path like tiny furry missiles, birds shouting at me from the hedgerows, and at one point, what I'm fairly sure was a fox giving me side-eye like I owed him money.

A couple more miles on those ever-reliable chalky tracks — where your tyres bounce just enough to keep you humble — and at long last, I could see *The Sustainability Centre,* just north of Chidden. Victory! Sanctuary! Enlightenment! And... oh look. It's next to a sewage *works*. Wonderful.

Nothing says "eco-conscious tranquility" quite like the faint whiff of recycled poop drifting on the breeze. Still, I was too tired to care. I'd made it. I was alive. And if the composting toilets didn't kill me overnight, I might just count this day as a win.

Arriving at the centre, I was greeted by a peaceful, eco-friendly vibe, the gentle smell of woodsmoke, and a field so dry it could've been auditioning for a role in *Mad Max: Hampshire Edition*. It wasn't always so zen, of course — during the war, this place was called HMS Mercury, and staggering in looking like I did would probably have got you court-martialled, shot, and then politely told off for soiling Her Majesty's gravel. But times have changed. These days, it's all windchimes, solar panels, and volunteers called Willow. The friendly staff — hippy types with suspiciously serene auras — gave me the once-over, winced ever so slightly, and then cheerily pointed me towards my pitch. Which, by total coincidence I'm sure, was located conveniently *downwind* of the office. Can't imagine why. Maybe they just thought the perfume of eau de cowshit and mild despair added to the rustic charm. Either way, I stank like a slurry pit in a heatwave and no amount of wholesome vibes was going to un-toast their nasal passages. Cycling up and down hills can do that to a man, apparently. Or a woman.

The ground was *rock solid* — some sort of post-apocalyptic, sun-baked substance that laughed in the face of tent pegs. I tried hammering them in like a man who still had hope. I now have several bent pegs, two bruised fingers, and a tent that looks like it was pitched mid-earthquake by someone with no depth perception and a grudge against geometry.

By the time it was up — if we're being generous with that definition — I was a walking case study in tactical failure. My legs didn't bend, my back had seized up like a Victorian factory, and I smelled like the inside of a cyclist's sock drawer. Seeking solace, I headed to the shower block, hoping for a rejuvenating rinse. The water pressure, however, was more of a gentle suggestion than a forceful stream. It was like being licked clean by a disinterested cat. Still, it was water, and after a day of cycling and swearing at tent pegs, I wasn't about to be picky. I managed to splash off the worst of the trail dust and remove most of the twigs from my hair, which I hadn't realised were there until I tried towel-drying and came out looking like a middle-aged scarecrow on a gap year.

The site was full of cheerful, barefoot hippy types, who all looked like they knew how to make their own hummus and communicate with bees. They were building yurts out of recycled teabags or something equally wholesome. Then came the real horror: *children*. Everywhere. Screaming, running, shrieking, somehow sticky despite being in a field. My exhausted brain processed it all as one long high-pitched blur of noise and peril.

I trudged up to the reception hut, looking and smelling like I'd just crawled out of a badgers' union meeting, and asked where the nearest pub was. The staff, bless them, rattled off their recommendations with the breezy confidence of people who have very clearly been to all of them. Many times. Possibly that day.

I followed their directions, which, miraculously, were accurate (hippies, it turns out, make excellent pub scouts), and ended up in a little local gem of a pub, where I was served *the* most glorious meat and potato pie known to mankind. It was hot, hearty, and unapologetically northern in spirit, if not in kind. Washed down with a pint of local beer that tasted like roasted dreams, I nearly wept with joy. I probably looked feral, but no one said a word. I like to think they thought I was a misunderstood poet. More likely, they assumed I was a very sweaty vagrant with a passion for carbs.

Either way, I'd earned that pie. And if I had to crawl back to my artistically wonky tent and fall asleep to the sounds of windchimes, composting toilets, and feral children communing with nature — so be it.

Chidden To Gumber Bothy

Day 2. Grass, Gravity, and Grudges

I awoke slowly the next morning, emerging from my tent like a particularly arthritic butterfly. The transformation from crumpled sleeper to sentient human followed the traditional Four Ages of Man. First came *Early Ape*, in which I lay flat on my back, blinking at the tent ceiling, unsure who I was or why my hip felt like it had been used to store rocks. Then *Bent Caveman*, crawling out into the dewy morning like I was auditioning for the role of "Man Who Regrets Everything."

Eventually, I graduated to *Grunting Homo Erectus*, making my way to the toilet block while dragging my toothbrush and muttering dark things about everything, including the dew, the floor, and the noise children make when they apparently stop needing sleep at 4:30am. Finally, I reached *Modern Human*, complete with clothing, caffeine cravings, and a burning desire for petty vengeance. And so, with toothbrush in mouth and a twinkle of retribution in my eye, I proceeded to zip and unzip my panniers with theatrical flair. Loudly. Repeatedly. I rustled bags. I clanged tent poles. I whistled. Screw you, night-goblins. If I can't have sleep, *no one* can.

Ready for breakfast, I wandered hopefully towards reception, only to be told with far too much cheerful serenity that, *"We don't serve food in the mornings, but there's some organic muesli in the honesty box."* I didn't want honesty. I wanted bacon. Or toast. Or revenge-based granola. Instead, I gnawed on a bar of compressed sadness while tackling the next challenge: tent peg extraction.

Now, remember how the soil had been harder than granite the night before? Well, now it had fully set into some sort of geological supermaterial. I pulled and twisted and nearly gave myself a hernia trying to liberate the bent little demons, which now resembled miniature boomerangs forged in the fires of spite. One of them shot out with such force I'm pretty sure it achieved low orbit.

Then came the sleeping bag. Oh, the sleeping bag. A deceptively fluffy object that expands with the confidence of a toddler in a tutu and *refuses* to return to the sack it came in. I folded. I rolled. I cursed. I even tried the desperate knee-pin-and-squeeze method. By the time it finally surrendered and went back into its impossibly small stuff sack, I looked like I'd wrestled a badger into a wetsuit.

And with that, I packed up the last of my dignity, threw my leg back over the bike, and pedalled off eastwards. Slightly broken, mildly unwashed, but fuelled by caffeine, passive-aggression, and the memory of that glorious meat and potato pie.

I rolled away from the Sustainability Centre with the optimism of a man who'd forgotten how much uphill there still was to come. The morning air was fresh, the light golden, and the lane I was riding down could've been plucked straight from a Visit England brochure — hedgerows bursting with life, wildflowers nodding gently in the breeze, birds singing like they were getting paid by the note. It was glorious. Idyllic. Practically cinematic.

And then I opened my mouth.

Big mistake.

Within seconds, I'd ingested what I can only assume was the entire cast of *A Bug's Life*. Midges, flies, one particularly chunky thing with legs — it was like nature had looked at my lack of breakfast and thought, *"Don't worry, mate, we got you."*

I coughed. I spluttered. I made noises not usually heard outside of veterinary emergencies. But hey, at least I wasn't hungry anymore — just mildly traumatised and possibly poisoned. A bonus protein boost with a side order of despair. It's hard to feel majestic while gagging on a wing and wondering if you've just swallowed something that glows in the dark.

Still, onward I pedalled. Full of vitamins, regret, and the kind of facial expressions that cause passing ramblers to give you a wide berth.

After the previous day's rolling horror show of hills, flies, and composting toilets, I was thrilled to find that the path heading east was — wait for it — *flat*. Actually flat. Not "flat if you ignore the bits that aren't," but properly, gloriously, sit-back-and-let-your-knees-have-a-moment flat. It traced the contours of a long, scenic stretch of hills, like the trail itself had decided to let me have a lie-in on two wheels. It was calm, quiet, and possibly the most civilised stretch of countryside since someone invented hedgerows. For about a hundred metres. Then it was bloody hilly again.

The plan was to take a short detour into Clanfield to find breakfast, ideally something greasy, healing, and medically inadvisable. But then, like a mirage rising from the land of sausage dreams, I stumbled upon the Roundhouse Café at *Butser Hill* — a scenic gem in Queen Elizabeth Country Park, and possibly the only place on earth where you can eat bacon while sitting next to a replica Iron Age house *and* a group of retirees arguing about hiking socks.

Butser Hill, by the way, is no ordinary mound. It's the highest point in Hampshire (271 metres of pure smug) and an official dark sky site, which means at night it becomes a hotspot for stargazing nerds who turn up with telescopes the size of canoes and get excited about nebulae. It's basically Glastonbury for people who think Orion's Belt is a thrill ride.

And if all that wasn't enough, Butser Hill has *showbiz credentials*. The Only Fools and Horses episode *Three for Tea* was filmed here — yes, *the* Butser Hill. It's the one where Del Boy gets roped into trying hang gliding, presumably because someone told him it was like falling with confidence. In true Del Boy fashion, he ends up launching himself off the hill with all the grace of a wardrobe in a wind tunnel, flapping and yelling while Rodney and Uncle Albert look on in horror and/or mild amusement.

So as I sat there, enjoying my full English breakfast with all the dignity of a labrador at a barbecue, I gazed out over the same hilltop Del once "flew" from. And the breakfast could've fed a minor battalion. The lovely girl behind the counter took one look at my dirt-smeared, bleary-eyed appearance and gave me extra everything, probably assuming I was on day 17 of a tragic survival documentary. Either that or she thought I was homeless. As I wolfed it down, a table of clean, well-moisturised, non-sweaty people watched me with a mix of concern and morbid fascination, like they'd spotted a feral animal using cutlery for the first time.

It was the breakfast of champions, or at the very least, the breakfast of a man whose previous evening was spent fighting tent pegs and children in a field next to a sewage works. Fueled by sausage, tea, and just enough shame to keep moving, I rolled on. Eastwards. Toward whatever fresh nonsense awaited.

And while you'd *think* — in your sweet, naïve little brain — that reaching the highest point of the route would mean it's all gloriously downhill from here... oh no. Bless your optimism, but no. The South Downs laughs in gradients. Downhill? Don't be ridiculous. This is where the trail really leans in, cracks its knuckles, and mutters "Hold my organic cider." Pity you, fool.

Heading south from Butser Hill, the trail turned into a completely different beast — *grass*. Not the nice, firm, manicured kind that makes you feel like a Tour de France legend gliding into Paris. No, this was *bouncy grass*. Springy. Rebellious. The kind of surface that turns your tyres into pogo sticks and your stomach into a washing machine.

Which, let's remember, was now full to the

brim with sausage, beans, black pudding, and enough toast to dam a river. My entire digestive system was being gently yeeted around as I rattled downhill like a human smoothie.

To make things more thrilling, the descent was *steep*, my brakes were as dependable as a 1990s dial-up modem, and the trail was helpfully scattered with *loose livestock*. Sheep doing existential stares in the middle of the path. Horses pretending they don't see you. It was like an English safari, except instead of a jeep I was on a clanking death tricycle and instead of binoculars I had panic in my eyes and crumbs in my beard.

By the time I dipped under the A3 — a surreal moment of suddenly hearing the whoosh of cars and remembering the outside world existed — I emerged into the heart of *Queen Elizabeth Country Park*. And boom. *Civilisation.*

The visitor centre was heaving with *normal people*. Clean people. People who smelt like soap and didn't have chain oil on their shins. Children were screaming about ice cream, parents were saying things like "Use your indoor voice!" and there was someone walking what can only be described as a dog in witness protection. It had legs like broomsticks, a jaw that jutted out like it was trying to escape, and a face like it had been assembled by committee during a power cut.

I'd survived grass, gravity, and livestock — but

nothing prepared me for the shock of re-entry into this caffeinated chaos. Still, it was good to know I was back among the people. I just wished I didn't look — and smell — like I'd crawled straight out of an Iron Age compost heap.

I didn't hang about at the visitor centre. I wasn't in the mood for food, crowds, or another child shouting *"Mummy, what's that man covered in mud eating out of a pannier bag?"* I nodded at a dog that may or may not have been a cursed sock puppet and made a swift, silent exit.

Once back on the trail, the path turned into something entirely more delightful: *woodland*. Proper, leafy, birdsong-and-dappled-light forest. It was like pedalling into a Nature Valley advert, minus the granola and with more midges. After hours of chalky trails, hills, and open exposure, it was a blessed change. Cool shade, a soft trail under my wheels, and best of all — *flat*. Sweet, merciful flatness.

But just when I was starting to believe the universe had forgiven me, I encountered the *next* faction in Britain's great countryside conflict: *pedestrians*. Not the friendly ones who smile and wave and say things like "Lovely day, isn't it?" No, this was a phalanx of pensioners, deployed like a Roman infantry unit with walking poles and passive-aggressive auras.

They saw me coming. I saw them seeing me

coming. And yet, when the narrow path made it clear *someone* had to give way, they stood their ground like I was trying to cycle through a family funeral. One of them, a woman with the expression of someone who'd just bitten into a lemon and found socialism inside, barked, *"You should give way to us!"*

So I stopped. Politely. Smiling the sort of smile that says, "I'm far too tired to be arrested today." As they shuffled past me, swarming in slow motion like beige-clad cattle with matching sun hats, I muttered, *"Absolutely, no problem at all. Age before Lycra."*

They didn't laugh. I didn't care.

To be fair, *everyone else* I'd passed all day had been lovely. Friendly walkers, cheerful hikers, even a couple with a dog that looked like it could do taxes. But this lot? Cyclist Kryptonite. I let them pass, feeling like a heron trapped in a puddle of ducks, and once the dust had settled and the scent of Werther's Originals had cleared, I carried on.

I mean, what *was* I supposed to do? Bludgeon them all with a tyre lever and bury them in the woods under a pile of pine needles? Apparently, that's "frowned upon" in modern society. Bloody political correctness. You can't do *anything* these days without someone piping up about "morality" and "basic human decency." Honestly, it's health and safety gone mad.

Anyway, after this, the trail left the trees... and went *uphill*. Not a gentle incline. No. This was the kind of hill that makes you question your entire belief system. Trees had bowed out, probably in solidarity. It was steep, relentless, and long enough for an existential crisis or three. So I did what any seasoned cyclist does in these moments: I got off and pushed, wheezing softly like an asthmatic accordion, while wondering if those pensioners were somewhere laughing behind me. Bastards.

As I neared the top of the hill, I ignored a sign that pointed to Buriton, but the village is just a few hundred yards to the north through the chalk pits if you are desperate for a pint, or a toilet, or a duck pond.

If you do go, you will find a charming little corner of Hampshire where the ducks run the show, the church is older than most countries, and the most scandalous event in living memory was when someone reversed *anti-clockwise* around the village pond. With a population of around 736 (as of the 2001 census, because apparently no one's checked since), it's the kind of place where everyone knows your name, your shoe size, and which hedge you were sick in after the last village fête.

Buriton *used* to be the important place around here. Back in the day, it was the posh big sister to Petersfield — before Petersfield got a railway station and Buriton got ghosted like a clingy ex. The reason? The slope was too steep for Victorian train engineers who presumably preferred their locomotives flat and emotionally stable. So while Petersfield got progress, Buriton was left on the platform waving a lace handkerchief and muttering, *"It's fine, we didn't want your fancy steam-powered nonsense anyway."*

Nowadays, Buriton is a designated sanctuary for ramblers, cyclists, and history nerds in waterproofs, all drawn by the bucolic charm and the chance to mutter reverently about Edward Gibbon. Yes, *that* Edward Gibbon — the man who wrote *The History of the Decline and Fall of the Roman Empire*. He lived here, presumably because it was the only place quiet enough to finish a multi-volume chronicle of the collapse of Western civilisation without being interrupted by a Deliveroo scooter.

I scooted on, however, enjoying the charms of a chalky track once again, interrupted only by the delights of farms and fields. I think I went into some kind of autopilot mode, and when I came out of it, for some reason which I could not fathom, I was lying on the floor.

My bike was next to me, with the back wheel spinning at an impressive speed, and then, ever so slowly, it came back to me what had happened.

It was a beautiful moment. The sun was

shining, the birds were chirping, the chalky path ahead was glowing with rustic promise — and I was gliding along like a man who thought, *"Yes, I've got this cycling thing absolutely nailed."* Confidence was high. Arrogance, higher. Speed? Questionable, but felt heroic at the time.

And then, just ahead, hidden in the soft white shimmer of chalky glory, lay the *Pothole of Destiny*.

I hit it at just the right angle — that magical, stupid angle — where your front wheel decides it's done with your nonsense and stops, but your body very much doesn't. Time slowed down. My arms flailed in a dramatic flourish. A squirrel in a nearby hedge audibly gasped. If there had been a trapeze artist nearby, they would've applauded.

I soared over the handlebars with the elegance of a man who has never, ever stuck a landing. I was a human trebuchet. A Lycra-clad meteor. A flailing, airborne warning sign to all who dared cycle with confidence.

Then came the inevitable: the *slide*. Chalk, meet knee. Elbow, meet gravel. Pride, meet abrupt and public demise. I skidded across the ground like a cheese wheel in a Cotswolds race, coming to rest in a cloud of dust, bad decisions, and the kind of silence that screams, *"You idiot."*

After a few seconds of lying there like a poorly parked mannequin, I did the standard cyclist's first response: looked around to check no one had seen. Luckily, only a horse in the next field bore witness, and judging by the way it walked off, it too was embarrassed for me.

My leg was bleeding — nothing dramatic, just enough to look like I'd lost a duel with a rogue bramble. And this, finally, was the moment I got to use the *first aid kit I almost didn't pack because it was 'probably unnecessary'*. I patched myself up using one plaster, two antiseptic wipes, and seventeen swear words.

Then came the bike. My mudguard had folded in on itself like a disappointed parent, and one of my brake cables had decided to retire early. I spent a good ten minutes fixing it with the grace and poise of a man doing keyhole surgery with a spoon.

Eventually, bruised, dusty, and with slightly less dignity, I was back in the saddle. Slower. Wiser. Slightly bloodier. But still moving — because while pride may be fragile, the lure of finishing the damn ride (and eventually sitting down again) is eternal.

My goal today, by the way, was Gumber Bothy — the South Downs' answer to "I want to feel like I'm wild camping, but I also enjoy a roof, running water, and not being eaten alive by things with more legs than me." It's remote, rustic, and ever so slightly smug. And honestly? I'm into it.

Tucked away in the middle of nowhere, Gumber

Bothy is the kind of place you have to walk or cycle to, which means you automatically earn points for simply arriving. You can't drive there. You have to *commit*. This isn't just a place to stay — it's a *statement*. A statement that says: "I'm outdoorsy, but not in a 'dig a latrine and eat moss' sort of way."

The bothy itself is a converted farm building, now lovingly equipped with bunks, a communal kitchen, and — *praise be* — proper toilets and showers. It's basic, sure, but that's the point. You're meant to be one with nature, not checking your 5G signal while reclining on a memory foam mattress. Though if someone did sneak in with a kettle and a duvet, I wouldn't judge.

It's peaceful. It's remote. It's surrounded by more wildlife than you can shake a biodegradable spork at. And when night falls? Oh, it's dark. Like, *dark dark*. Lose-your-shoe kind of dark. Perfect for stargazing, or lying awake questioning your life choices while your sleeping bag audibly crinkles every time you breathe.

It was still a fair slog to go, so I carried on, ever the optimist, foolishly thinking the trail had exhausted its supply of surprises. Spoiler: it had *not*. From here on out — pretty much all the way to Eastbourne, actually — the path sashays dramatically along the top of the South Downs, treating you to sweeping views on both sides like some sort of smug geographical catwalk.

To the north, you've got the Weald of Sussex, or just *the Weald* if you're trying to sound local and mysterious. It's basically the flattish bit sandwiched between the North Downs and the South Downs — a sort of scenic no-man's land, but with more garden centres. And to the south? That'd be the English Channel, which, as the name subtly hints, is indeed... a channel. Full of water. Separating us from France. You're welcome for that GCSE-level geography refresher.

Next up was a little diversion to South Harting, or as my inner 12-year-old insists on calling it: *South Farting*. Yes, I know, I should be more mature — but come on. The name practically begs to be giggled at. And beneath its unfortunately flatulent-sounding title lies one of the most surprisingly posh, eccentric, and culturally overloaded villages on the South Downs Way. It's like someone dumped a sack of historical celebrities here, gave them a pub and a parish church, and said, "Now behave."

First up, *Peggy Guggenheim*. Yes, *that* Peggy — the eccentric American art collector, wearer of enormous sunglasses and questionable hats, and someone who made a career out of funding surrealists and drinking martinis before noon. She lived in South Harting during the 1930s, presumably because even art world royalty needs a break from Paris and scandal. She was the daughter of Benjamin Guggenheim who went down with the Titanic in 1912 which left her with more cash than she could imagine. One can only imagine her swanning about the village, confusing the locals with her avant-garde jewellery and habit of casually owning Picassos.

And then there's *H.G. Wells*, who occasionally lived up at Uppark House while his mum worked there as a lady's maid. Imagine little Bertie Wells (Herbert George), future father of sci-fi, running around the grounds and soaking up inspiration for *The Time Machine* while probably being told off for muddy boots. I like to think he invented interplanetary travel just to escape from being made to tidy his room.

As if that weren't enough intellectual heavy lifting, along comes *Bertrand Russell* and his wife Dora, casually founding an experimental school at Telegraph House in 1927. It was called *Beacon Hill School*, and it was the kind of place where maths was optional but free thought was compulsory. Bertrand was all about logic, philosophy, and upsetting the establishment — so obviously, he settled in South Farting and brought progressive education, arguments, and probably a lot of beige cardigans with him.

Let's not forget *Anthony Trollope*, the Victorian novelist who spent his twilight years in the village writing the kind of deeply English fiction where nothing happens, but it happens with great social consequence. His pen, paperknife and *letter scales* are proudly displayed in the parish church, which is either incredibly quaint or the literary equivalent of keeping someone's Fitbit in a shrine.

Oh, and just to round things off, you've got Admiral Sir Horace Law — because what's a proper English village without a retired naval officer turned lay preacher — and Cliff Michelmore, the iconic 1960s TV presenter, buried here next to his equally glamorous wife Jean Metcalfe. Because even the *dead* in South Farting have celebrity credentials.

In short, South Farting may sound like a digestive issue, but it's actually a cultural hotspot stuffed with dead philosophers, surrealist patrons, and Victorian novelists.

South Farting isn't the only little gem of a place-name along the South Downs Way, however, but we'll get to them later, because now we have more history to discover, and that is Uppark House.

If you're in desperate need of a break from the relentless up-and-downery of the trail, this wonderful stately home is just a short detour away — and absolutely worth the effort. Not just for its stately Georgian architecture, its beautifully manicured gardens, or its sweeping views across the South Downs, but because, let's be honest, it has *toilets*. And *food*. And seating that isn't a rock.

By this point in the journey, I would have sold a kidney for a sandwich that hadn't been lovingly steamed in my backpack for six hours. So yes, history is lovely, but flushing loos and a National Trust café? That's the real heritage experience.

And while you're there, take a moment to soak in the gloriously bonkers history of the place. Uppark was originally built in the late 1600s for Ford Grey, the 1st Earl of Tankerville — a man who sounds less like a nobleman and more like an underperforming hatchback. It was later bought by Sir Matthew Fetherstonhaugh, whose surname is pronounced, I kid you not, *"Fanshaw."* Because of course it is. Why pronounce all the letters when you can ignore three-quarters of them and confuse everyone?

Sir Matthew, being a man of means and very questionable spending habits, buggered off on a Grand Tour of Europe to buy art, antiques, and probably syphilis, before coming back to redecorate Uppark in the fashion of someone who wanted *everyone* to know they'd been to Italy. His son, Sir Harry Fetherstonhaugh (still pronounced *Fanshaw*, still refusing to make sense), spent much of his life throwing parties, fathering children with the help, and generally living like a Georgian rock star. Then, at the ripe old age of 71, he shocked absolutely no one by marrying his 21-year-old dairymaid, Mary Ann. True love? Possibly. Mid-life crisis with added milk? Almost certainly.

When Sir Harry finally died — presumably from exhaustion or sheer incredulity — Mary Ann inherited the whole estate and passed it on to her sister, who then handed it to two friends, but *only* if they changed their surnames to Fetherstonhaugh. Because apparently, owning a stately home wasn't enough — you also had to pretend you were named after a sneezing fit.

And just to keep things spicy, a young H.G. Wells used to hang around Uppark while his mum scrubbed the floors—probably dreaming up time machines while nicking biscuits and rummaging through the library. There, he devoured revolutionary texts by the likes of Thomas Paine —Lewes local, professional troublemaker, and the man who basically handed America its independence with one angry pamphlet and a quill.

Oh, and in 1989, a careless workman set the house on fire with a blowtorch. Obviously. But thanks to a frantic rescue effort and the slightly manic dedication of the National Trust, Uppark rose from the ashes like a very well-insured phoenix, and now stands proudly once more, ready to offer you a slice of cake and a clean loo. Which, frankly, is all I ever want from history.

I didn't stay too long, what with smelling and looking like something that cat had dragged in, and was soon back on the trail where I immediately saw another little nugget of history.

Vandalian Tower is South Farting's towering tribute to ambition, fantasy, and a complete inability to read the geopolitical room. Perched proudly (and slightly pathetically) atop Tower Hill, this crumbling cylinder of stone was built in 1774 by Sir Matthew Fetherstonhaugh — whose name sounds like a sneeze and whose grasp on colonial success was, let's say, *optimistic*. He constructed the tower to celebrate the glorious future British colony of *Vandalia* — a land that would one day be... well, *nowhere*.

That's right. Vandalia — planned to sit somewhere in what's now West Virginia — was supposed to be the Crown's next big American conquest. Spoiler alert: it never happened. The British government basically looked at the proposal, blinked, and went, *"Yeah, we'll get back to you."* Then the American Revolution kicked off, and suddenly the whole "let's build a new colony" plan looked a bit... deluded. So Vandalia went the way of Blockbuster Video and powdered wigs: grand in theory, tragic in execution.

So now we have the Vandalian Tower: a monument to a colony that never existed, built by a man who thought, *"You know what would look great on this hill? A big stone cylinder to celebrate a total failure."* It's the architectural equivalent of getting a tattoo of your ex's name the day before they dump you.

But wait, there's more — this historical masterpiece is also known as *Lady Hamilton's Folly*. Emma Hamilton, famed mistress of Lord Nelson and general 18th-century scandal magnet, supposedly used the tower to watch for Nelson's ship coming into port. Nothing says "eternal love" like climbing a ruin in your corset and heels to spot your sea-bound boyfriend while he's off sinking things and probably catching syphilis, apparently.

In the end, the tower burned in 1842 — because of course it did. And it was only stabilized in the 1980s by people who clearly didn't have Netflix yet. Today it stands as a crumbling, moss-covered lesson in unchecked optimism, colonial fantasy, and really bad planning, and ironically is fenced off to protect it from... vandals.

Go visit it. Take a selfie. Marvel at the absurdity. Just don't ask what it's for, because the answer is: absolutely *nothing*.

The path through Farting Wood, sorry, Harting Wood was one of those deceptive stretches where your brain keeps going, *"Oh, this is flat,"* while your legs scream, *"LIAR!"* It wasn't properly hilly, but it certainly wasn't flat either — more like a relentless series of undulations designed by someone who enjoys watching cyclists question their life choices. The trail sort of flirted with the contours — up a bit, down a bit, twisty enough to make you suspicious, but never quite committing to a full-on climb. It was like being gently mugged by topography.

Then, just when I was settling into a rhythm and my thighs had stopped sulking, it happened: *Beacon Hill.* Yes, *another* Beacon Hill. Because apparently every county in England has at least three, and all of them are uphill, smug, and waiting to ruin your day.

I don't know who named them, but I suspect it was a sadist with a fondness for elevation and a total lack of imagination. "What's that? A hill you can see things from? Call it Beacon Hill!" *Again.* Cheers, Dave. Real creative.

So, off we go again — upwards, obviously. Because the South Downs Way doesn't believe in plateaus. Only pain.

At one point, the path took a mysterious lurch to the side — like it had suddenly remembered a dentist appointment — and I stopped to check the map, suspicious. Because nothing says "fun day out" like a random detour in the middle of nowhere when your legs already feel like overcooked linguine. I squinted at the route, certain that this must be some cruel mistake or a mapping error created by someone drunk on contour lines.

But then, a revelation: the detour was there

to *go around* the hill. *Around it.* Not over. Not up. *Around.* It was, in that glorious moment, the most beautiful curve I'd ever seen. I could have kissed the map, if it wasn't already soggy with sweat and covered in snack residue. With renewed enthusiasm, I took the turn, cheerfully following the path around the base of the hill like a sensible person with a strong sense of self-preservation, and a deep distrust of unnecessary altitude.

And so I courageously carried on — or at least something vaguely resembling courage, powered mostly by stubbornness, crumbs, and the faint hope of a pub sometime before the next ice age. The miles began to creep up, slowly, reluctantly, like they too were feeling the burn. The path, which had once graciously meandered through woods and gentle gradients, now decided to embrace its inner sadist. It got twistier. Sharper. And, most offensively, *hillier.*

Suddenly, every turn seemed to reveal another incline, rising up before me like a smug geological prank. My strategy, if you can call it that, was to hurl myself downhill with the grace of a startled wheelbarrow, then use the leftover momentum to *hopefully* sling myself partway up the next climb. It worked... sometimes. Other times, I simply came to a dramatic, wheezing halt halfway up and had to do the Walk of Shame, pushing my bike and trying to pretend I was just "taking in the view" and "connecting with nature" instead of praying for death or a conveniently placed escalator.

Eventually, I arrived at *Devil's Jump* — which, fun fact, is not one mound but a whole *family* of them. A weirdly enthusiastic collection of lumpy earth, like someone started making barrows and just didn't know when to stop. Maybe the Devil himself popped by with a wheelbarrow and a bad attitude. Either way, it felt like the kind of place where history, myth, and exhausted cyclists all come to lie down for a bit and rethink their decisions.

I didn't so much as jump off here, but fall off, and decided to make a break of it and brew up a coffee. With sugar. And chocolate. And sugar.

The Devil's Jumps, are an ancient collection of five perfectly pleasing Bronze Age barrows, strutting their stuff in a neat little line across the South Downs like they're auditioning for *Britain's Next Top Tumuli*. Seriously, they've been sitting there for over 3,000 years, refusing to crumble or blend in, just vibing with the landscape and screaming, *"We were here before your Saxon nonsense, thank you very much."*

And the name? Oh, it's not just a quirky nickname. According to local folklore (which, as we all know, is 10% truth and 90% pub-fuelled embellishment), these mounds were the personal playground of *the Devil himself*, who apparently got bored one afternoon and decided to start leapfrogging over ancient burial sites. As you do. Unfortunately, he chose the wrong postcode to play silly buggers in, because *Thor* — yes, actual Norse thunder-god Thor — took one look at this nonsense and chucked a celestial boulder at him. Boom. Devil gone. Cue dramatic exit, stage left.

Now, you might think that's a weird blend of mythologies — why is Thor popping up in a story about the English countryside? Well, nobody know, but who cares! This is folklore. It doesn't need continuity, it needs *chaos*.

Astronomers also love these mounds because they line up with the midsummer sunset, which means your Bronze Age ancestors were out here building celestial calendars while we're still arguing about daylight savings time. Imagine hauling earth to make a sacred site that aligns with the solstice, and thousands of years later some Lycra-clad idiot (hi, it's me) cycles past and says, *"Huh, weird little bumps, aren't they?"* Because that's what they are. Good for having a picnic on, though.

The path dragged on like a hungover sloth-twisting, turning, sulking up hills and tripping down the other side — and somewhere along the way I stumbled across a rather large, somewhat knackered-looking boulder. For a brief, hopeful moment I wondered if it was a glorious glacial erratic, dropped here centuries ago by a grumpy retreating ice age. But no. It was chalk. And not just any old lump of chalk, oh no — this was apparently a *sculpture* by someone called Andy Goldsworthy. Now, I don't want to sound uncultured (I absolutely do), but in my book, a sculpture is supposed to vaguely resemble *something*. A person. A dog. A confusing abstract metaphor, maybe. But this? This was a rock. That looked like a rock. Carved to resemble — itself. Art, darling!

And the best bit? He got *paid* for this. Not just once — there are fifteen of these things littered around the place. Fifteen! That's not a sculpture trail, that's a scam with scenic views. Someone, somewhere, signed off on this and probably said the words "transformative use of natural form" without choking. Meanwhile, I'm over here covered in mud, smelling like a dead sheep, wondering how I missed my calling as a professional rock rearranger. Maybe I *am* just a philistine. But at least I'm a philistine with a functioning bullshit detector.

But there was more madness to come. A quick check of the map told me I was almost at one of the craziest places in the country, though one that most people have never heard of.

Let's talk about *Monkton House* — a place so gloriously unhinged, so delightfully bonkers, that it makes your average stately home look like a beige filing cabinet. Hidden away in West Dean, and about one hundred yards from where I now stood, this was never *just* a house. No. This was a surrealist explosion of wealth, weirdness, and what happens when someone says, "What if we built a house... but made it *absolutely feral*?"

Originally designed in 1902 by posh-architect-to-the-elite Edwin Lutyens as a shooting lodge (because god forbid rich Edwardians have to shoot pheasants without architecture), it was later taken over by Edward James — trust fund surrealist, moustache enthusiast, and the kind of man who looked at Salvador Dalí and said, *"Mate, hold my absinthe."*

Edward James didn't just redecorate. He transformed Monkton into Britain's only *complete* surrealist house. The outside had fake bamboo drainpipes and fibreglass palm trees, because subtlety was obviously outlawed. Inside? Oh, just casually padded walls (for the emotional support, one presumes), a carpet patterned with the footprints of his Irish wolfhound (which had previously been adorned with his ex-wife's), and furniture that looked like it escaped from a Salvador Dalí fever dream (because it had). And yes, of course the infamous Lobster Telephone and Mae West Lips Sofa lived here (Dali again). Because nothing says "have a seat" quite like smooching furniture and seafood-based telecommunications.

It wasn't a house, it was a *meltdown in bricks*.

A place where dreams, delusions, and "why not?" came together, threw a cocktail party, and did a shed load of drugs.

Naturally, in the 1980s, it was all auctioned off, because Britain has a long tradition of selling off its most gloriously deranged treasures when someone at the Trust runs out of cheddar. The surrealist furnishings, many by Dali, were scattered to the wind, and the house now lives on as a private residence — presumably full of wallpaper that actually matches itself and furniture that doesn't flirt with you.

Still, if you're ever hereabouts, pause for a moment. Somewhere behind this hedgerows lies a house where surrealism once dropped acid, hired an architect, and redecorated with a sense of reckless, glorious abandon, and is probably only place where answering a phone might get you pinched by a lobster.

Sadly, there was nothing to see through the trees, and not wanting to get arrested for trespassing, I carried on.

Up ahead, and just a short diversion off my route, was another delight of a village and one with an even better name that South Farting. This was Cocking, and was where I went next, in search of food, but not before I had to wrestle with Cocking Hill and Cocking Down. Literally everywhere around here, apparently.

Welcome to Cocking — yes, *Cocking*. Go on, get the giggles out of your system now, because this innocent little village nestled in the South Downs has been putting up with your childish smirks since the Domesday Book. It's pronounced just how you think it is, and no, the locals are not amused by your witty "I came through Cocking and didn't feel a thing" commentary.

But behind that gloriously unfortunate name lies a village with a weirdly star-studded, delightfully unhinged history.

First, let's talk *industry*. In the 19th century, Cocking was home to the Chorley Iron Foundry, a place that forged metal goods and, weirdly, the future of New Zealand politics. One of their apprentices was Charles "Carlino" Brown, the son of *actual poet bestie* Charles Armitage Brown (mate of John Keats, literary heartthrob and consumptive cough legend). Carlino ditched Cocking and its foundry, headed off to invent a tobacco slicer, and then accidentally became a senior New Zealand politician. Because obviously, that's the natural career path from "rural forge" to "international statesman."

Then there was the Cocking railway station, opened in 1881 with high hopes and shut in 1935 with a weary sigh after almost no one used it. By 1953, a freight train derailment — caused by a spectacularly washed-out embankment — put the final nail in the tracks. Today, it's a private house, probably with excellent acoustics for muttering *"we could've been Brighton."*

But wait, Cocking wasn't done being weird. Enter the Cocking Lime Works, in operation since 1715, where people not only burnt lime but also, apparently, risked spontaneous death. Case in point: William Marshall, tragically squashed by a chalk pit earthquake in 1833. Yes, an actual earthquake. In Sussex. In a chalk pit. Honestly, the universe *did not like him.* And if that's not strange enough, the 1861 census helpfully informs us that a tramp named James Bennett was discovered *living inside a lime kiln.* Because who needs a house when you can sleep in what is essentially a Victorian pizza oven?

Cocking is like one of those tiny English villages that looks completely innocent, but then you dig a little deeper and discover it's got more plot twists than a BBC crime drama. Train disasters, literary connections, industrial tragedies, rogue earthquakes, political refugees — it's like *Downton Abbey*, but with more lime and worse train service.

What I really wanted, though, apart from my food, was a selfie of me and the road sign. I got it, too, but I also got some funny looks from the locals.

The final couple of miles to Gumber Bothy were less a gentle roll to the finish line and more a final test of physical endurance, emotional stability, and my willingness not to launch my bike into a hedge and live in the woods forever. First of all, there was the horrible hill out of Cocking.

It began, as these things so often do, with a road. Not just any road — oh no. This one was somehow even *narrower* than the last, which I previously thought was only passable by woodland creatures and cyclists with very low self-esteem. This new lane seemed to exist purely to give passing cars the thrill of potential vehicular intimacy and me the creeping dread of ending up in a hedge while mouthing the words *"I have a bell, please don't kill me."*

Eventually, I escaped the clutches of the tarmac and rejoined the familiar crunch of chalk track beneath my wheels, winding through a stretch of lovely, leafy woodland that might've been serene if I wasn't so profoundly knackered. Trees arched above like nature's version of a pity hug, birds chirped like motivational speakers who'd never ridden a bike in their lives, and the trail continued its now-customary approach of "not quite uphill, but definitely not flat either."

Just past Upwaltham, a sign pointed off to Gumber Bothy — a short detour that felt suspiciously like someone whispering, *"Go on, just a little further... we promise it's there."* I turned off, eyes half-closed, legs functioning on blind hope and muscle memory alone, and rolled into the bothy like a man who had seen some things. I was sunbaked, sweatcrusted, mildly traumatised by hills and livestock, and held together mostly by crumbs and spite.

But I had made it. Gumber Bothy. A sanctuary. A safe haven. A place where I could collapse in the most dramatic way possible and not be judged for smelling like despair.

Checking in at Gumber Bothy was easy enough. I wheeled myself in like a sweaty parcel marked *'Handle with Caution'* and was met by a friendly member of staff, which was nice — until I was immediately attacked by a cat. It leapt out from behind a bench and wrapped itself around my ankle like a fluffy landmine. Mildly startled and now sporting a light bleeding, I mentioned this to reception who blinked, smiled politely, and said, *"We don't have a cat."*

Right. Brilliant. So either I hallucinated it from exhaustion, or Gumber Bothy is haunted by the ghost of a feral tabby with boundary issues. Either way, I moved on.

I was then directed to pitch my tent in the field *over there*. "There" turned out to be roughly seven miles from the showers. Honestly, I think I passed a different postcode on the way. By the time I reached the allocated grassy square of solitude, I was too tired to argue. I pitched my tent — *still wonky*, but no longer resembling modern art — and for once, the ground's concrete-like hardness was a bonus. As I hammered in the pegs with the subtlety of a blacksmith having a tantrum, they somehow straightened themselves back into shape.

Then came dinner. I unpacked my JetBoil stove and began the sacred ritual of *burning absolutely everything I touched*. My fingers, the food, the pan, possibly part of the grass. Whatever I was trying to make tasted exactly like carbon, but it was hot and it didn't argue with me or run away, so it counted as a win. I chased it down with a cup of coffee — if you can call bitter, gritty caffeine sludge brewed in semi-darkness a "cup of coffee" — while being joyfully eaten alive by insects. It was a buffet, and I was the main course.

Thankfully, no children tonight — just the gentle ambiance of several *very* stinky hikers snoring like cartoon lumberjacks in the distance. It was oddly comforting. I crawled into my slightly-less-wonky tent, zipped up the door, and was asleep the second my face hit the inflatable pillow. Either that or I passed out from heatstroke and JetBoil fumes. Either way, I remembered nothing. Bliss.

Gumber Bothy To Truleigh

Day 3. Flat Tyres and False Hope.

I woke up to discover I had a blister. On my foot. This annoyed me. I wasn't walking, I was cycling, so how this happened was beyond me.

But what annoyed me more was that I also woke up to the soft, soothing patter of rain on the tent — nature's way of saying *"Good morning, fool. Everything you own is now damp."* Around me, the chorus of snoring hikers and cyclists continued in full surround sound, as if they were auditioning to be the wind section in a phlegmy brass band. It was oddly peaceful, if you ignored the part where I had to get up and exist in it.

Still, priorities: *coffee*. Which I brewed inside my tent like the reckless idiot I clearly am. Pro tip — unless you're parked within sprinting distance of a fire station, don't try boiling water inside a small nylon box filled with flammable materials and yesterday's socks. The JetBoil hissed like an angry snake, condensation gathered ominously on the ceiling, and for a brief moment, I genuinely thought I might be the first person to be airlifted out of Gumber Bothy for accidental espresso-based arson.

Once sufficiently caffeinated and only lightly steamed, I began the misery that is packing away in the rain. Every single item had gained three pounds of wetness overnight. The tent was like folding a sponge. My clothes stuck to me in places I don't want to talk about. My sleeping bag tried to escape. And then — *as I zipped the last pannier* — the rain stopped. Just like that. Gone. The clouds parted, the sun peeked out, and somewhere in the distance, I'm sure I heard nature laughing.

And there, sitting silently on a patch of grass, was the cat. You know — the one that doesn't exist. Back again, watching me pack with unblinking intensity, like it was the regional manager of doom. It was clearly hungry. Possibly possessed. Definitely still a bastard.

I nodded at it. It blinked slowly, as if to say, *"I'll see you tonight. You smell like tuna."* Then I pedalled off, damp, dishevelled, and followed — probably — by a cat-shaped omen.

After surviving the feline poltergeist of Gumber Bothy, dodging rainclouds, and narrowly avoiding boiling myself alive in my tent, it was time to rejoin the South Downs Way. To do that, I pedalled off via Stane Street — an ancient Roman road, which, to be honest, is just a very fancy name for "the oldest cycle path in Britain that absolutely wrecks your backside."

Stane Street, for those not currently brushing up on their GCSE Latin, was the Romans' idea of a shortcut from Chichester (then delightfully known as *Noviomagus Reginorum*, because even back then, they couldn't resist naming things like a spell from *Harry Potter*) to Londinium, which of course is modern-day London, now with fewer togas but significantly more coffee chains.

The Romans, being Roman, didn't believe in bending roads gently around hills or rivers or anything inconvenient like *nature*. Oh no. They were all about straight lines. If a mountain got in the way, they'd probably just raise an eyebrow, stab it with a spear, and keep going. And so Stane Street slices its way through the countryside like a giant stone ruler laid down by someone with a severe case of control issues and no concept of gradients.

To be fair, it was impressively well-built: aggermound in the middle, ditches on either side, compacted gravel, flint, and what I can only assume was the crushed morale of whichever poor sods had to build it. Riding it today, you get a real sense of history... mostly through your spine. The path is a blend of flinty bumps, ruts, and the occasional suspicious wobble that makes you wonder if this was once a chariot pile-up.

But despite the bone-rattling, I had to admire it. The Romans really *committed*. They even had rest stops — *mansiones* — which were basically service stations without the KFC, placed every 15-20 miles for changing horses and refueling on olives or wine.

And now? That same route carries tired walkers, grumpy cyclists, and probably the occasional confused Deliveroo driver. So as I bounced along this ancient engineering marvel, thighs burning and tyres complaining, I tipped an invisible helmet to those sandal-wearing lunatics who carved a motorway across southern England, just so we could all suffer gloriously on it two thousand years later.

Cheers, lads. You really knew how to lay a road. Just next time — maybe throw in a bench. Or a flat bit. Please.

Having rejoined the South Downs Way, I was promptly and enthusiastically greeted by a long, energy-sapping hill — the kind that rises in that smug, slow gradient that says, *"You thought this would be easy, didn't you, you naïve breakfast-less fool."*

It was *early*. Too early for uphill anything. And I hadn't even eaten yet, unless you count chewing on your own bitterness. I gave it a valiant go — pedalled for all of twelve seconds — before hopping off and trudging up like a dishevelled pack mule on a gap year. This happened several times: ride, wobble, despair, walk. Repeat. I was basically playing a one-man game of *Willpower vs Gravity*, and gravity was winning by a total knockout.

Eventually, I made it to the top. Legs shaking, blood caffeine-free, and powered only by stubbornness and rage. But the view? Oh, the view. The clouds had parted, the sun had reappeared like a smug influencer after a digital detox, and I could suddenly see for miles. Rolling hills, patchwork fields, maybe even my soul briefly leaving my body and floating toward the next village in search of toast.

My plan — nay, *my dream* — was to get breakfast in Amberley. A village I now regarded less as a destination and more as a shining beacon of fried hope. After a quick breather and a dramatic lean on a fencepost, I threw myself back on the bike and began to freewheel downhill, feeling like the wind was finally on my side.

And then it happened.

Not a pothole this time. Not a rabbit. No, my own drivetrain decided to betray me mid-swoop. One moment I was flying, the next I was skidding sideways, flailing like a man trying to unicycle on an oil slick, and then — *boom*. Off the bike. Again. Just a few scratches, no broken bones, luckily, just the usual bruised ego and a healthy coat of dust, gravel, and mild shame.

For a full five, I was crouched in the grass, swearing inventively, fingers slick with chain oil, trying to un-jam a chain that had jammed up during an ill-timed gear change. Nothing says *great start to the day* quite like a mechanical breakdown, mild personal injury, and the looming realisation that you still haven't had any toast. Oh, and I trapped my finger. Ouch.

Amberley had better have bacon.

If you're the kind of person who gets weak at the knees over a good bit of Roman grouting, then you might fancy a short detour to Bignor Roman Villa — home to some of Britain's best-preserved mosaics and, allegedly, *"the finest Roman mosaic floors in Northern Europe."* Which is a bold claim. Very bold. Especially considering they've clearly never been to *Hull* and seen the absolute *banger* that is the Rudston Swastika mosaic at the East Riding Museum. That thing's a masterpiece. It's Roman. It's intact. It's got geometry so sharp it could slice your GCSE confidence in half. Oh, and it's got a Swastika.

But back to Bignor. The villa was discovered in 1811 when a farmer ploughed straight into ancient history — nothing says "welcome to heritage" like wrecking it with a plough. What followed was the unveiling of a sprawling Roman estate complete with underfloor heating (naturally, the Romans were too posh for cold toes), fancy dining rooms, and miles of mosaic flooring, which — let's be honest — were basically ancient brag rugs.

One of their proudest features is a 79-foot mosaic corridor, which they've described with almost indecent enthusiasm. It's long, it's intricate, and it's mostly people in sandals doing questionable things with grapes and spears. Sure, it's impressive. But let's not pretend it's the *only* mosaic worth shouting about. The aforementioned Rudston Swastika — now proudly housed in my home town of Hull — has everything: design, drama, historical controversy, and the added excitement of making tourists very uncomfortable until they read the sign explaining it's 1,800 years old and *not* a tribute to 1930s Germany.

Anyway, if your thighs aren't burning too badly and you're the kind of person who thinks a tile-based detour is better than a bacon sandwich, then by all means — swing by Bignor. Me? I'll be cycling straight past, dreaming of breakfast and silently defending Hull's right to Roman mosaic glory.

What goes up must come down — and in my case, it came down wheezing, rattling, and praying my brakes didn't give up mid-sentence. The descent from Bignor Hill was less of a relaxing roll and more of a chalky death luge peppered with random undulations. The track couldn't decide if it was a path, a pothole collection, or a geological tantrum. One minute I was gliding like a Tour de France legend, the next I was bouncing over craters large enough to host a village fête.

Somewhere in the chaos, I passed a couple out walking. She was power-walking ahead with the energy of a woman who had *had enough*, while he trailed behind wearing the expression of someone who'd just been told he was holding the map upside down since breakfast. Not a word passed between them, but their body language screamed, *"He forgot the anniversary and said something stupid about her mum."* Honestly, I should've offered him asylum.

As the path continued its identity crisis — flip-flopping from smooth to shattered like a tarmac version of a mood swing — it finally dropped down into the glorious Arun Valley, where the town of Amberley came into view, smugly picturesque and annoyingly charming, like it was curated by the National Trust and styled by a Jane Austen theme park. And interestingly, if you have had enough of potholes and biking, Amberley has a train station that will whisk you straight to London. Just saying.

Amberley is one of those places that looks like it's permanently ready for a photo shoot. Over 70 listed buildings, each one more "oh wow, is that original brickwork?" than the last. It's got a castle (obviously), now a swanky hotel, because nothing says "historic fortification" like a champagne breakfast and underfloor heating. And nestled around it, cottages that look like they've been personally fluffed by antique dealers.

Then there's the River Arun, winding through the village like a moody teenager. It's one of the fastest-flowing rivers in England, presumably because even the water wants to get out of West Sussex before the cream tea prices go up again. The Romans called it *Trisantonis*, which allegedly means "the wanderer," though I suspect it really meant "oops, not that way."

By the time I rolled into Amberley — mud-splattered, bruised, and still tasting chain oil — I didn't care about castles or cobbles or charming riverbanks. I wanted food. Hot food. Possibly an exorcism. But mostly, I wanted to sit somewhere where the ground wasn't trying to throw me into a hedge. Welcome to Amberley. Historic. Beautiful. Slightly smug. Just like everyone who lives there.

After a quick wander around the town — sorry, I mean the *"village"*, because despite all the cobbled charm and castle drama, it turns out this place is technically *not* a town (I know, devastating) — I set about my most important mission of the day: food.

Now, the dining options were... limited. We're talking "village-limited." There was a tea room, obviously, because you're legally required to have at least one in every picturesque postcode. There was a pub, but it was shut — probably due to some local emergency like someone misplacing their heirloom chutney. And then there was the train station, which offered what I can only describe as a sandwich that had clearly been there since Edward the Confessor popped in for a snack. Its ingredients were a mystery. I suspect the mould was extra.

So: tea room it was. I shuffled in, mud-smeared, oily, and smelling like a blend of despair and chain lube, and was seated in a corner far enough away to be polite but close enough that the pensioners could still tut within earshot. They looked at me like I'd just cycled in from Mordor, which to be fair, isn't entirely inaccurate.

I ordered the most reasonably edible-looking thing on the menu — a sandwich that cost roughly the same as a small car and a "pot of tea for one", which somehow managed to make me feel both hydrated and emotionally attacked. Around me, well-dressed retirees delicately nibbled scones and made passive-aggressive comments about the *"unusual aroma of the countryside."*

Sorry, Mavis. That's not the countryside you're

smelling. That's me. Cyclist-à-l'orange, freshly sautéed in sweat, mud, and trail regret.

Still, overpriced or not, it was food, it was hot(ish), and no one physically removed me from the premises. A solid win all round. And one of the staff told me I was halfway along the route. I'm not sure if that was good or bad.

After politely scalding my mouth on my pot of tea and traumatising the local pensioners with my eau de cyclist funk, I had a quick look at the map — mostly to figure out where I was heading next, but also to delay standing up again. And that's when I was struck by a mildly inconvenient truth: I had absolutely no idea where I was sleeping tonight.

There were a few camp sites scattered vaguely along the route like breadcrumbs left by a forgetful hiker, but whether I'd actually make it to one of them? That was up for debate. It all depended on how my legs held out, whether the weather behaved, and whether my bike decided to spontaneously eject parts again like it had done previously. So the plan was simple: just keep going until I either found a campsite or collapsed dramatically in a hedgerow and claimed squatter's rights.

With that little existential crisis shoved back into the saddlebag of denial, it was time to move on. Which, of course, meant one thing and one thing only: up. Because the South Downs Way isn't happy unless it's making you cry in low gear. Honestly, this trail's definition of "forward" is *upwards with attitude*. Dammit.

To my surprise — and mild suspicion — the path out of Amberley (sorry, *village*) actually started as a well-tarmacked road. I know. Smooth surface. Actual grip. It felt suspiciously like cheating. But before I could get too comfortable, I realised it came with a trade-off: hordes of hikers. Honestly, it was like a queue for a National Trust gift shop had broken loose and taken to the hills. Fleece jackets, walking poles, conversations about flapjack portions — *everywhere.*

But as I climbed — because of course it was uphill, why wouldn't it be — the crowds began to thin out. First the kids disappeared (probably bribed with ice cream to turn back), then the casual walkers gave up, and eventually, even the hardcore hiking couples vanished, leaving only silence, sweat, and the distant wheeze of my own lungs. And cyclists? There were none. Because most people aren't stupid enough to cycle up a chalk cliff, dragging a half-tonne of camping gear behind them.

But then — finally, *finally* — the top. The moment my legs had cursed me for since breakfast. The path levelled out, and suddenly the whole world cracked open: a 360-degree panorama of rolling hills, distant villages, and more sky than you could reasonably process without a drone licence. It was breathtaking. Literally. I'd just spent forty-five minutes gasping up a vertical white slope like an asthmatic llama. But it was worth it. For a few glorious minutes, I forgot my burning thighs, my questionable breakfast, and the fact that I still didn't know where I was sleeping. The view was the kind of payoff that makes you say, "Yeah, alright. You win, South Downs. You smug, beautiful beast."

The next stretch felt... *endless*. Not in a spiritual, transcendental, "I became one with the trail" kind of way — more in a "how is this still going?" kind of way, as I pedalled along a chalk path hemmed in on both sides by fencing, like some sort of two-wheeled livestock being gently herded across the top of the South Downs.

To be fair, the views were glorious. Rolling hills in one direction, patchwork fields in the other, the occasional dramatic swoop of a red kite overhead, and no sign of civilisation apart from the ever-reliable trig points and the odd smell of manure wafting on the breeze. Blissfully remote. Blissfully quiet. Almost *too* quiet.

Somewhere near the summit of Kithurst Hill, I began my noble (and futile) quest to find the legendary rusting tank that had, for decades, been quietly decomposing in the undergrowth like a forgotten tin of corned beef. A World War II

Churchill tank, no less — left behind after military training, parked up like someone had popped to the shops and never came back. It had become a sort of accidental war memorial, a beloved rust bucket watching over the Downs, providing excitement for hikers and, I assume, nesting opportunities for several generations of confused birds.

But could I find it? Could I hell.

I looked. I squinted. I stared at lumps in the landscape with hopeful, increasingly desperate energy. Was that it? No, just a suspiciously angular bush. What about that? Nope, someone's aggressively square dog. And then I found out — *after* the fact, naturally — that the tank had already been removed. Removed. Just spirited away like a rusty Cinderella at midnight. No fanfare. No plaque. No helpful sign saying, "Sorry, your tank has been relocated due to being *too interesting*."

Apparently, it had been stripped for parts by souvenir hunters over the years (because of course it had — who wouldn't want a 70-year-old bolt as a paperweight?) and then — get this — it was lovingly winched off the hill and *sent to a museum in France*. France! Like Britain didn't already have enough museums, or hills, or need for tanks that double as outdoor furniture.

So here I was, tankless, betrayed, and trudging

along in a mist of bitter disappointment. Honestly, I felt personally targeted. I'd been dreaming of a dramatic, windswept photo next to a hulking, rusting war machine — a sort of "gritty historical Instagram influencer" moment. But no. All I got was an empty field, a bruised sense of trust, and yet another reminder that life is, at its core, deeply unfair.

I didn't see many people up here — just a few distant specks of walkers far off on the ridges, like ants with hydration packs. But there was one couple, all smiles and woolly hats, out with their dog. A medium-sized mutt with a twinkle in its eye and, as it turned out, a burning hatred of bicycles. It took one look at me, snarled like it had just remembered a childhood trauma involving stabilisers, and *launched*. Full-speed, teeth-baring chaos. I pedalled like a man trying to escape his sins.

The owners, breathless and useless, yelled the usual lines — *"He's never done that before!"*, *"He's just curious!"*, and my personal favourite: *"He doesn't usually like men!"* Like that's somehow better? I didn't hang around to clarify whether they meant male humans or just *me* in particular, but I'd wager it was the combo of Lycra, panic sweat, and pure fear that set him off.

Once I'd outrun Cujo and my heart rate had dropped below emergency levels, the path mercifully followed the northern edge of the Downs. For once, the trail resisted the urge to throw me up and down hills like a sadistic fitness app. It was reasonably level — undulating, sure, but not in that "let's ruin his soul" kind of way — and stayed that way all the way to a point just south of Washington.

And just to be clear, that's *Washington, West Sussex*, not the one with the Capitol Building, nuclear arsenal, and lobbyists. No, this one has a petrol station, a pub, and possibly the same number of potholes.

There's a little detour you can take into Washington village — probably for food, or tea, or some sort of sanity. But no, not me. I powered on like a noble idiot, continuing upwards and onwards, heading for the one and only Chanctonbury Hill. A place shrouded in myth, magic, and mist (depending on the weather) — and home to a very special secret, which we'll get to... right after my journey was brought to a dramatic, grinding halt by the first great inevitability of cycle touring: the puncture.

Of course it was going to happen. We all knew this moment was coming. But punctures don't show up when you're resting in a shady picnic spot with good phone signal and morale. Oh no. They arrive halfway up a hill, far from everything, when your water's low, your thighs are twitching, and your soul has already started writing its resignation letter.

I stopped, dismounted like a broken cowboy, and assessed the damage. Rear tyre. Obviously. Because if a puncture's going to happen, it might as well hit the one that's hardest to remove, change, and put back on without swearing in multiple languages. I gave it a look and found the culprit: a thorn. Not just any thorn — this thing looked like it had been fired from a medieval ballista. It had *layers*. It had *attitude*. I'm pretty sure it had a postcode.

Luckily, I'd come prepared. No dramatic patch kit moment for me — I just whipped out a spare inner tube like a jaded magician, swapped it in, checked the tyre like a crime scene investigator, and was back up and running within minutes. Covered in oil. Slightly feral. But mobile.

Chanctonbury Hill still lay ahead, mystery intact, and now I was armed with a slightly more cynical mood and one less inner tube in reserve. What could possibly go wrong next? (Please don't answer that.)

The next stretch was very hilly — and not in a charming, rolling countryside sort of way. No, this was the kind of hilly that makes your legs file formal complaints and your bike creak like it's reconsidering your entire relationship. I gave it a go, of course. I always do. But after a few heroic attempts at pedalling up inclines that looked suspiciously vertical, I gave in and walked. Or rather, *shoved* — because my bike, weighed down with gear and resentment, had suddenly developed the grace of a reluctant fridge.

Eventually, sweating profusely and questioning my sanity, I crested what I *thought* was the summit and looked ahead with joy in my heart and lactic acid in my legs... only to discover that Chanctonbury Fort — the tree-lined, magical, mystical destination I'd been dragging myself toward — wasn't actually on Chanctonbury Hill.

No. Of course not.

It was just past it, like some mythical finish line that keeps moving the moment you get close. Because apparently, on the South Downs, there is *always* further to go. Always.

But I made it. At long last, I stumbled into the clearing near the fort, dropped my bike like a sack of emotional baggage, and flopped to the ground in a glorious, gravelly collapse. It was peaceful. Almost spiritual. A well-earned rest with views for miles and a gentle breeze kissing my sweaty forehead.

Then a bird of prey — some magnificent feathered maniac — swooped overhead and let out a screech that sounded suspiciously judgemental. Honestly, it felt personal. Like it had clocked my

Lycra and decided to file a complaint with the local wildlife committee.

Still, I was here. I'd earned it.

Local legend has it, if you run around the ring of trees seven times anticlockwise, the Devil himself will appear and offer you a bowl of soup in exchange for your soul. Because, apparently, the Prince of Darkness moonlights as a soup kitchen manager. The specifics vary — some say it's porridge, others insist on milk — but the consensus is clear: accept the bowl, and you're in for a hellish afterlife.

But the Devil's culinary endeavors don't stop there. Another tale suggests that if you manage to count the exact number of trees in the ring — a task deemed impossible due to some magical trickery — you'll witness the ghostly march of Julius Caesar's legions across the Downs. I mean, fair enough, nothing says "haunted hilltop" like a Roman military parade.

And if spectral soldiers and demonic soup vendors aren't enough, Chanctonbury Ring is also a hotspot for UFO sightings, phantom horses, and even a lady on a white horse. It's as if the hilltop couldn't decide on a theme and just went with "all of the above."

Once I'd finished communing with the Devil (or more accurately, sitting near a spooky clump of trees while eating a flapjack), it was time to get moving again. The trail resumed its usual trick of "following the contours of the hills" — which sounds nice on paper but basically means it *pretended* to be flat by snaking around the slopes like a drunk snake with commitment issues.

The track was quiet now. Eerily quiet. Probably because it was getting late. Everyone else with common sense had already reached their destinations, set up camp, ordered a pint, and were probably halfway through their lasagne while I was still chasing the sun across chalk ridges like a budget adventurer with no time management skills. The silence was beautiful, though. Just me, the wind, and the occasional disgruntled bird who clearly didn't appreciate Lycra.

I started thinking about camping. You know, in that vague, panicky way where your brain says "We should find somewhere soon" but your legs are like, "Let's just see if the next hill is *maybe* not terrible first." That kind of logic.

Then, just as I was mentally negotiating with myself over which bush I'd be willing to sleep behind, the path took a sudden, dramatic plunge — the kind where you start descending before your brain catches up and realises you're basically freefalling on two wheels. Down I went, skidding and swearing, into another river valley.

This time it was the River Adur, a name that

sounds less like a river and more like a spell someone yells in a fantasy novel. It's got that slightly odd, vaguely mystical energy that makes you wonder whether it's going to flow normally or suddenly summon a water nymph with attitude.

I zipped through the little village of Botolphs (yes, that's a real name, not a typo or a rejected Harry Potter house), which was quiet, sleepy, and looked like it hadn't seen a cyclist since the invention of rubber. It was charming, in a "blink and you miss it" kind of way — though I nearly didn't blink at all because my eyes were still watering from that descent.

Time was ticking, the sun was slinking toward the horizon, and I still needed somewhere to camp. But for now, at least, I was back in a valley... which usually means only one thing: the next bit is *definitely* uphill. Again. Of course it is.

I rolled to a stop beside the River Adur, both to give my brake pads a moment of silence and to do a quick assessment of my situation — which, at that moment, could best be described as "uncertain with a chance of panic." I had light fading fast, no confirmed campsite, and a body held together largely by flapjack crumbs and hope.

I pulled out the map, squinted at it like it had personally insulted me, and looked at my options. There were a few small towns to the north, which was cute, but unless I fancied stealth camping behind a Co-op or spooning a recycling bin, they weren't offering much in the way of overnight charm. No campsites. No pubs with gardens. Just the creeping dread of "oh god, where am I going to sleep?"

And then — glory.

A little icon popped up on my phone like the digital voice of salvation: YHA Truleigh Hill. A youth hostel. With beds. And walls. Possibly even electricity. The kind of miracle that only a tired, half-broken cyclist can truly appreciate. It might as well have said "Spa retreat and emotional support centre."

The fact it was called Truleigh Hill just made it sweeter. Yes, truly, this was truleigh good news. (You're welcome. I'll see myself out.)

Suddenly, the world seemed brighter. The chain oil didn't sting as much. Even my saddle sores wept with relief. A hostel meant food. Showers. A mattress not made of tree roots and shame. I still had to get there, of course — and given the name, it was very obviously going to be *uphill* — but for now, I had a destination, and that was enough to pedal on with renewed enthusiasm. Or at least slightly less despair.

So off I went, up towards Truleigh Hill, legs groaning, gears grinding, and hope clinging on like the last Pringle in the tube. I was picturing the warm glow of a youth hostel window, maybe even a vending machine that didn't sell just sadness, when I saw them: cyclists coming the other way. Two of them, cheerful enough, until I asked the fatal question — "Is the hostel open?"

They gave each other a look. You know the one. The look people give before delivering terrible news like *"we're out of bacon"* or *"your fly's been down all day."*

"It's full, I'm afraid," one of them said, shaking his head with genuine sympathy.

Full.

The word hit like a flat tyre in the soul. I nodded and smiled like I was totally fine with it — "Oh, no worries, of course, that's cool, I love sleeping in hedgerows like a Victorian tramp" — but inside, my brain was quietly screaming into a pillow.

Still, I had no choice. I carried on. What else was I going to do — live under a stile?

Darkness was falling now, wrapping around the hills like a damp cloak. The track blurred into shadows, and every rustle from the bushes sounded like a big scary monster was hiding within them. I pedalled on, fuelled by a heady cocktail of desperation, fatigue, and the faint smell of my own socks.

And then — there it was. The lights of the

YHA Truleigh Hill hostel, shining like a beacon of moderately priced salvation. I rolled into the courtyard just in time, the last of the daylight evaporating behind me like a theatrical curtain drop. It felt dramatic. It felt cinematic. I probably looked like a badly lit zombie arriving at the reckoning. But on a bike. And smellier.

Maybe they were full. Probably. But maybe — *maybe* — they'd let me camp outside. Just a corner of grass. A patch of dirt. Somewhere to collapse with dignity (or at least privacy). I could still use the facilities. Maybe even have a shower that didn't involve rain or crying.

I'd made it. Truleigh Hill. Truleigh miraculous.

I dumped my bike against the low wall outside the hostel like a weary cowboy ditching his horse at the saloon and staggered inside, one saddle-sore short of a full breakdown. Behind the reception desk stood Gavin — smiley, welcoming, and, crucially, not holding a pitchfork or a "NO VACANCY" sign.

"Hi," I croaked, "I don't need food. I've made my peace with starvation. What I *do* need is somewhere to wash and then lie unconscious for about twelve hours."

He chuckled in that *"oh, we've had your type before"* sort of way, then paused. "Food's finished for the night anyway, I'm afraid."

"That's fine," I nodded, heroically. "I'll simply perish slowly. You carry on."

But what I was really interested in was whether I could pitch a tent somewhere, because — *as I'd been told* — the hostel was full. Gavin frowned and paused. "Full? That's odd. We're not full."

Cue a short, awkward silence while my brain processed this new, possibly glorious information. I explained that two hikers I'd met earlier had said the place was booked out. That seemed to flick a switch in Gavin's brain.

"Ah," he said. "They asked about a shared dorm bed. *That's* full. But we've got *loads* of private rooms."

So, to recap: they weren't full at all. The two hikers just didn't want to spend the extra few quid on a room and were planning to go wild camp in the bushes like budget wombles. I, meanwhile, took the room faster than you can say 'card or contactless,' practically floated to the shower, and finally got clean enough to be in the same room as myself again.

Refreshed and significantly less feral, I wandered into the lounge and got talking to two women cycling the other way, looking just as knackered but far more organised. Mel and Kim (yes, really) had wine, were ordering pizza, and, best of all, didn't mind sharing either. One minute

I was feral bike-dad on the brink of collapse, the next I was sipping cheap rosé and inhaling garlic bread like I'd just emerged from a bunker.

And just like that, the day ended the way all good cycling days should: full, clean, warm, a little tipsy, and surrounded by people who understood why you smell like a goat that's been through an apocalypse.

South Downs Way, Day Whatever: complete.

Truleigh To Eastbourne

Day 4. Eastbourne or bust. Preferably Eastbourne, but let's keep our expectations flexible.

I woke up early, mostly out of some bizarre sense of determination but also because my body had fully given up on sleeping after three days of abuse. I stumbled into the shower, which managed to be both tiny and absolutely freezing, and then treated myself to a surprisingly good — and very reasonably priced — full English breakfast. By this point in the trip, I was so calorie-deficient I probably would've eaten the menu if it had gravy on it, but this was the real deal: eggs, bacon, beans, the lot. Bliss.

Then came the traditional morning wrestling match with my sleeping bag, which still refused to go quietly into its compression sack. We fought, it swore at me in polyester rustles, I elbow-dropped it into submission, and eventually I won. Just. I was grateful to have had a roof over my head, not least because it had absolutely *lashed* it down during the night. Everything outside looked like it had been through a spin cycle on "apocalypse."

With my gear packed and my dignity mostly intact, I went to check on the bike. And of course — *of course* — there it was. A flat tyre. Because what better time for a puncture than right before setting off on the final day? Cheers, universe. Much appreciated.

Still, if you're going to fix a flat, doing it next to a warm B&B with access to tea and mild swearing is about as good as it gets. I whipped out my last spare inner tube — yes, the *last* one, because apparently bringing two for a four-day ride was me being wildly overprepared — and did the old tyre change shuffle. Hands filthy, spirits medium, I patched it up, crossed all available fingers, and rolled off with the confident optimism of a man who definitely knew he had no more backup plan.

The trail, bless it, had really upped the stakes for the finale. Not content with simply being its usual bumpy, rut-riddled self, it had now added a luxurious layer of slippery mud and a pothole filling system known in technical terms as "giant puddles of mystery depth." Lovely. Everything was soggy, slippy, and completely primed to throw me off the bike like a particularly spiteful rodeo bull.

But hey — sunshine, optimism, and just the mild threat of catastrophic mechanical failure.

What could possibly go wrong?

I'll tell you what could go wrong — *another* bloody flat tyre. Barely a mile or two in. Overlooking the gloriously named village of Fulking. Fulking Hell, obviously.

Honestly, the optimism didn't even make it past the first hedgerow before reality came crashing in with a slowly deflating tyre. Apparently, in all my mechanical genius, I'd failed to properly check the inner tube I'd just triumphantly fitted. And no, this wasn't another prehistoric thorn unearthed by the gods of trail sabotage — this time it was a rusty nail. A nail. On a chalky farm path. Where from? Did an 18th-century carpenter lose his satchel here mid-renovation?

So there I was, once again, crouched on a patch of damp grass, getting a cold, wet arse for my troubles, wheel in one hand and all hope rapidly draining out of the other. Thankfully, it was the front tyre, so at least I didn't have to take half my bike apart this time.

I had no spare tubes left, however, so it was time to go full old-school, patch repair mode. Fifteen miserable minutes of rubber fiddling — yes, it sounds wrong, and yes, it *was* — before I finally got the thing reassembled, re-pumped, and re-attached, all while muttering a selection of words not found in any polite cycling handbook.

At long last, I was back on the bike. Again. Fingers crossed. Again. Spirits? About as soggy as the weather.

Which brings us back to Fulking, because we can't just let that one go, can we? Hell no. It's called *Fulking*, for crying out loud — it practically begs for attention. And just when you think the name alone is doing all the heavy lifting in the comedy department, it gets better. Because Fulking was historically part of the *rapes* of both Bramber and Lewes. Yes. *Rapes*. What? Indeed, *what*?

Now, if you're sitting there blinking and wondering whether someone misread a medieval scroll while half-cut on mead, you're not alone. A *rape*, it turns out, was the name for a subdivision of the ancient county of Sussex. Because apparently, in the olden days, "parish" was far too basic, and even "wapentake" — which sounds like a Viking party game — wasn't quite bizarre enough. No, they went full chaos and landed on *rape*. I can only imagine how that village meeting went:

"Right lads, we need a name for this new administrative region. Something solid. Memorable. Future-proof."

"Well, how about something deeply unfortunate that'll make history teachers, tourists, and innocent cyclists recoil for centuries to come?"

"Excellent idea, Geoff! We'll call it a rape!"

I mean, was this the same naming committee responsible for Fulking? Did they just gather once a year to ruin maps and scandalise modern guidebooks? Somewhere in Sussex, there was clearly a very bored monk with a quill and a wicked sense of humour.

So yes, Fulking. Once part of two rapes. It's a real place, with a real history, and I cycled through it with the maturity and composure of a ten-year-old spotting a rude word in a textbook. Which, frankly, is the only way to do it.

As it was, I really wanted to visit Fulking — just to see what all the Fulking fuss was about. But alas, I didn't have enough Fulking time, and there was that massive Fulking hill standing between me and Fulking enlightenment. And let's be honest — what goes down, inevitably has to come Fulking up again, and I was in no mood for that kind of Fulking rubbish. So I didn't bother. I just turned around, muttered a heartfelt "sod this Fulking nonsense," and Fulked right off.

Apologies. I couldn't resist. But I'm back now. Time to move on, I think.

The path was still soaking wet, like someone had tried to turn the South Downs into a slip 'n slide for masochists. I pedalled on with all the grace of a frightened deer on roller skates, nervously scanning the trail for anything that might a) burst my last remaining tyre, b) break me in half, or c) both. Every puddle was a potential deathtrap, every root a treacherous prank from the countryside. My entire body was clenched tighter than a Victorian vicar at a drag brunch.

And then, cresting a hill with thighs like jelly and dignity long gone, I found myself face to face with... *The Dyke Golf Club*. That's right. *The Dyke*. Golf. Club.

Now, I know what you're thinking. And shame on you. No, it's not a lesbian Satanist leisure centre. You filthy-minded deviant. It's named after the *Devil's Dyke*, which is an entirely innocent geographical feature and not, I repeat *not*, the Devil's long-lost Sapphic companion. Though frankly, I'd watch that Netflix series.

So what *is* the Devil's Dyke, apart from an endless source of immature snorts? Well, it's the UK's biggest dry valley, carved out during the last Ice Age when melting snow had nowhere to go and decided to dramatically erode its feelings into the landscape. Geologists say it's all to do with frost and gravity and erosion, but honestly, who cares about facts when we have folklore?

Legend has it that the Devil himself got into a strop because everyone in Sussex had found Jesus and were no longer available for eternal damnation or casual deals involving fiddles. So he decided to dig a trench from the coast to the Weald to flood the lot and teach them a soggy lesson. But just as he was mid-dig, some sneaky monk lit a candle and tricked a cockerel into crowing — because apparently poultry are sacred timekeepers now — and Old Nick thought dawn was coming, panicked, and legged it, leaving behind his half-dug dyke and a heap of mythical earth that now forms everything from the nearby hills to the bloody Isle of Wight. Overkill? Definitely.

Then came the Victorians, bless them, who looked at this majestic natural wonder and thought: "What this needs is *tourists* and *mechanical nonsense.*" So they chucked up a funfair, two bandstands, an observatory, and a camera obscura-because obviously the only thing better than a sweeping view is a blurry version of the same thing inside a wooden box. They built a train line to cart Londoners in their stiff collars and loathing of mud right up to the dyke's edge. And because hills are for peasants, they also installed a funicular railway *and* a cable car, because if there's one thing the Victorians loved more than gout and repressed emotions, it was overengineering things for fun.

Sadly, the tourist tat is long gone, but the dyke remains — a glorious scar in the land, steeped in history, myth, and accidental innuendo. If you don't at least giggle once while passing it, congratulations: you're either incredibly mature, or already dead inside.

Now if you'll excuse me, I've got more mud to eat.

After barely surviving the puddle gauntlet of Devil's Dyke with both tyres and dignity semi-intact, I rolled into a place that sounded like the beginning of a limerick and the end of my patience: Saddlescombe. Or as I'd been privately calling it for the past half hour — *Saddlesore*. Which, to be fair, felt far more appropriate considering what my backside was going through by this stage.

Now, Saddlescombe is one of those blink-and-you'll-miss-it hamlets that seems to exist solely so the postman can get his steps in. But here's the twist — it's got *history*. Serious, dramatic, Indiana-Jones-meets-Monty-Python history. Back in the 13th century, this unassuming little bump in the landscape was gifted to the Knights Templar. Yes, the mysterious sword-swinging monk-types who were either protecting the Holy Grail or hiding Dan Brown's next plotline. Imagine them riding through here in full armour, yelling things like "Ni!" and trying not to get stuck in the mud.

If you've got the time (and you should, because your legs could use the excuse), check out *Saddlescombe Farm*, a National Trust property with all the rustic charm and slight whiff of sheep you'd expect. But the real reason to go? The

Donkey Wheel. Yes, you read that right — a *Donkey Wheel*. It's basically a giant wooden hamster wheel, only instead of an adorable rodent doing cardio, it was powered by a donkey plodding endlessly to haul water from a well. Centuries of high-tech irrigation, and medieval Britain looked at the problem and went, "Get a donkey to walk forever." Genius. Also slightly sinister. I imagine the donkey HR department had notes.

So yes, don't skip Saddlescombe — sorry, *Saddlesore*. No, wait. *Saddlescombe*. The village. Not my medical condition. Easy mistake.

Another glaring oversight on my part has been failing to mention the gates. Yes — *gates*. Riveting stuff, I know. Strap in. Because apparently, I've decided to suffer in silence until now, when the cumulative trauma of the bloody things can no longer be ignored.

I haven't bothered to mention them up until now because, well — *they're gates*. Who gets excited about gates? "Ooh look, another wooden barrier designed to keep livestock from achieving their dreams." Riveting stuff. But the thing is, as the ride dragged on and my patience thinned to the consistency of instant gravy, it became increasingly difficult *not* to mention them. Because these gates — these smug little wooden tripwires — are bloody *everywhere*.

At first, it's fine. You dismount, unclip, swing

the gate open with a flourish, glide through like a country gent, and carry on your merry way. But by the 47th one, the novelty wears off faster than lycra in a bonfire. When you're on your own, it's a full-on routine: stop, get off, fumble with the latch (which is always either rusted shut or booby-trapped), wrestle it open without toppling over, wheel the bike through, shut the gate behind you (because heaven forbid a sheep tastes freedom), get back on, reclip, wobble into motion — and then, thirty feet later, do it *again*.

And don't get me started on the sheep. This stretch of the trail is absolutely *heaving* with the woolly little menaces. Staring at you with that blank expression like you've interrupted something important, chewing aggressively, loitering just long enough to make you prepare for impact. Dickheads.

So yes, the gates are annoying. But apparently, the alternative is free-range sheep launching themselves off hillsides and into traffic, so I suppose we all have to suffer for the greater good, and talking of which, enter Pyecombe, stage left.

Navigating Pyecombe was like playing a deeply traumatising level of *Frogger*, but rewritten by Quentin Tarantino after a bad breakup with a cyclist. Two A-roads. *Two!* Because apparently one high-speed roulette wheel of death wasn't quite murderous enough for the sadists who designed this bit of the trail.

The first road teased me with hope. It had a bridge — *a bridge!* Like civilisation had briefly remembered that cyclists exist and don't want to die. I trotted over it like some smug, windswept god of lycra, hips swinging, helmet shining, practically blowing kisses to the traffic beneath me. "Look at me," I thought, "riding above the chaos like the King of the Fulking Downs."

Then I turned the corner and got drop-kicked back to reality. The second A-road didn't *have* a bridge. It had *intentions*. Dark, bloodthirsty ones. No zebra crossing, no lights — just two lanes of sheer vehicular lust for destruction. I had to hobble across while dodging speeding metal boxes, each one piloted by someone who looked like they'd do unspeakable things to get their hands on a Clubcard meal deal and weren't about to let a lonely cyclist slow them down. I swear one driver made eye contact with me like, "You're the reason I pay insurance," and *gunned it*.

It was like trying to cross a motorway during the Hunger Games. I lunged, I yelped, I did what can only be described as a panicked shuffle-sprint-slither hybrid while clutching my handlebars like a rosary. If I were a cat, I'd be on my tenth life and applying for reincarnation.

I made it, somehow, fuelled entirely by blind panic and stubborn northern grit, and immediately fell half into a hedge, legs trembling, mouth swearing, and thoroughly traumatised. Sexy it was not. But alive. Just.

A short detour was in order, during which, thank the Gods, I only *almost* died once (which, statistically, is practically a success story by this point), and I soon arrived at the north portal of Clayton Tunnel — and I'm not being dramatic when I say it looks like a *fairytale castle built by a railway-obsessed wizard who'd just discovered LSD*. I mean, turrets? Gothic arches? And then, just for fun, someone whacked an actual *house* on top of it. Yes. A house. Sitting smugly on the entrance like it's guarding Narnia, but for trains.

It's the kind of architectural choice that makes you wonder whether the Victorian engineer in charge was genuinely brilliant or just catastrophically bored. "Gentlemen, we could just build a tunnel portal... or hear me out... we build *Camelot for locomotives*, complete with crenellations and a surprise domestic dwelling." And then nobody said no, because Victorians were off their chops on opium.

This majestic madness was built in 1841 and stretches over a mile and a half *beneath* the South Downs. That's right — while I was grunting and wheezing along the trail above, actual trains were zipping underneath me like smug, steel centipedes, probably carrying passengers who weren't wet, muddy, or wondering if their left butt cheek had stopped existing.

Now, this whimsical slice of railway history isn't *just* a giant set piece from a deleted scene in *Harry Potter and the Southern Rail Delay*. Oh no. It's also the site of one of Britain's most spectacular early train disasters — because of course it is. In 1861, thanks to a delightful cocktail of human error and "oh it'll probably be fine" logic, three trains ended up *in the tunnel at the same time — on two lines.* Oops.

What followed was a catastrophic pile-up that killed 23 people, injured 176 more, and presumably caused several bowler hats to be launched into orbit.

So, if you're ever in the area and fancy seeing a Disney castle that moonlights as a tunnel for high-speed death tubes, *Clayton Tunnel's north portal* is your spot. It's bonkers, brilliant, slightly cursed, and absolutely worth the detour — especially if you only get clipped by *one* car along the way.

After surviving this detour with only minor psychological scarring and just the one near-death experience (standard fare by this point), I found myself pedalling back toward the South Downs Way when — bam! — I was ambushed by two colossal windmills perched atop the hill like they owned the place. Meet Jack and Jill, the Beyoncé and Jay-Z of the Sussex milling scene.

Jill, the elder of the two, was born in Brighton in 1821 and was later hauled up the hill to Clayton in 1852 by a team of oxen. Yes, oxen. Because when you need to move a massive post mill five miles uphill, you call in the bovine cavalry. Jill is a post mill, which means the entire structure pivots to face the wind — a bit like a giant wooden ballerina with a gluten obsession.

Jack, on the other hand, is a five-storey tower mill built in 1866. Unlike Jill, Jack doesn't dance; he broods. He's the strong, silent type, towering over the landscape with a stoic presence. Interestingly, Jack is one of the few male-named windmills in the country. Most mills are considered female, but Jack breaks the mould.

But these aren't just pretty faces. Oh no. In 1861, Jack was the site of a grisly accident when a miller got a little too close to the machinery and met a rather unfortunate end. And during World War I, Jack's granary was used to manufacture airplane engines. Obviously.

Make sure you visit when passing. They're not just windmills; they're local celebrities with a flair for drama and a history as rich as the flour they once milled. Just watch out for the oxen — they've been known to hold grudges.

The next few miles were a full-blown emotional rollercoaster disguised as a bike ride. The terrain changed more often than a politician's stance during an election year. One minute I was elegantly coasting along like I was in an advert for sustainable living, all smooth paths and wind in my hair, and the next I was bouncing over rutted chalk like I'd entered the "Sod Your Spine Challenge 2025."

But then — *boom* — Mother Nature turned up the charm. To the north, the Weald stretched out like an Instagram filter made flesh: rolling fields, twee villages with names like Duckbottom-on-Weasel (probably), and smug little tea room that probably charge twelve quid for a scone and a frown. The sky had gone full Cornish postcard — deep, cinematic blue, not a cloud in sight — and every butterfly in Sussex had apparently received the memo. They were out in droves, flapping around like they were high on nectar and unpaid attention, the airborne equivalent of a hen do in Ibiza.

Somewhere along this scenic fever dream, I passed a couple of fellow cyclists — fit, friendly types who looked like they'd just pedalled in from a spa weekend. We shared a few pleasantries that translated roughly to: "You dying too?" "Absolutely." "Great stuff, let's pretend we're enjoying this." And off we went, bonded forever by mutual dehydration and trauma.

Then, disaster nearly struck. I was coasting

downhill, finally feeling like a competent human being, when out of the bushes *burst a horde of feral children*. Wild, barefoot, shrieking and completely untethered from civilisation — possibly raised by squirrels. They sprinted across the trail with zero warning, and I came *this close* to bowling one over like a rogue ten-pin. Not that I would've been hurt — they weighed about the same as my lunch — but let's just say that in that moment, the lack of number plates on bicycles became a feature, not a flaw. I had a solid getaway plan and a plausible story involving bees.

Eventually, somehow, I made it to the summit of Ditchling Beacon — a place that sounds like a scenic lookout but is actually a carefully disguised leg-murdering hell climb. At the top, I whipped out the Jetboil like a true outdoorsy legend and made myself a cuppa. That's right: tea at altitude. Like a posh Bear Grylls but with lower morals and more biscuits. I sat there with my steaming mug, legs twitching like post-traumatic jelly, gazing out at the ridiculous view across the Weald, feeling oddly victorious — but by victorious, I mean sweaty, dead inside, and slightly windburnt.

Still. No kids were flattened, tea was made, and the view was great. That, my friend, is what we call *a win*.

Perched at the top of Ditchling Beacon, clutching my steaming Jetboil brew like the post-apocalyptic barista I was born to be, I took a moment to soak in the view. Miles of rolling fields stretched out below like a giant green duvet, and dotted across it, some of Sussex's finest villages — each with their own little chunk of history, gossip, and unintentional comedy gold. And since I wasn't quite ready to face more uphill nonsense, I thought, *why not sit here and judge them from above like a caffeinated god?*

First up: Ditchling. Lovely little place. Famous for, among other things, being the birthplace of *Dame Vera Lynn*, the "Forces' Sweetheart" and World War II's answer to Adele. Best known for *"We'll Meet Again"*, which sounds comforting until you realise it's basically an emotional hostage note. She sang for the troops, raised national morale, and somehow managed to smile through the entire Blitz while most of us complain if Greggs runs out of steak bakes. Icon.

Next on the viewfinder: Camilla Shand. Don't recognise the name? Try *Camilla Parker Bowles*. Still no? Oh come on — *Queen Camilla*! Yes, the one who caused a royal scandal big enough to make *EastEnders* look tame. And would you believe it, she went to school right here in Ditchling, at Dumbrells. A posh boarding school where, reportedly, her room looked like a bomb site. Prophetic, really. Before she was swanning around Buckingham Palace, Camilla had a string of posh boyfriends (because of course she did —

this is Sussex, not Love Island), but her on-again, off-again, oh-look-we're-married-now thing with Prince Charles turned the monarchy into a soap opera for at least two decades. Honestly, the crown might be made of diamonds, but her patience? *Titanium.*

Pan a little east and you'll find Westmeston, home to *Raymond Briggs*, the man who emotionally traumatised an entire generation with *The Snowman.* Lovely tale. Boy meets snowman, snowman melts, child learns about loss. Merry Christmas! But Briggs wasn't just about melting misery. He also wrote *When the Wind Blows*, a charming little graphic novel about two pensioners slowly dying in a nuclear holocaust. Honestly, it's amazing he wasn't banned from Waterstones. The man had range — from whimsical airborne adventures to full-on Cold War nightmares. Respect.

So there I sat, slurping tea and roasting the countryside from 248 metres up, surrounded by butterflies, blue skies, and historical madness. Sussex: beautiful, bonkers, and full of people who either ruled the world, sang to it, or traumatised it with nuclear-themed cartoons. Delightful.

With my gear begrudgingly shoved back into its usual unwilling bags, I peeled myself off the summit like a man reluctantly leaving a nice warm pub to walk into a hailstorm of reality. Time was getting on, Eastbourne was still miles away, and I had all the urgency of a hungover tortoise. My legs were staging a mutiny, my backside had applied for asylum, and my water bottle had begun to smell vaguely like despair. Still, off I went, because no one else was going to cycle to the bloody coast for me.

Roughly five minutes later — because of course — what should appear on the horizon but a *charming little coffee van*. You know the sort: hand-carved sign, artisanal oat milk, possibly owned by someone named *Rainbow*. A lovely spot to sit, relax, and enjoy a hot drink... which would've been perfect *if I hadn't JUST HAD ONE ON THE TOP OF A MOUNTAIN LIKE AN IDIOT*. Nothing like smug, perfectly-timed refreshment to remind you that your life choices are poorly scheduled at best.

Still mildly bitter and deeply under-caffeinated (it's possible to be both), I glanced down across the peaceful green sprawl of Plumpton, which sounds like a character from *Postman Pat* but hides a secret more rock 'n' roll than anything your nan's ever knitted. Yes, believe it or not, this sleepy little village — home to racehorses, polite hedgerows, and the occasional awkward women's institute meeting — was once the stomping ground of none other than *Led bloody Zeppelin*.

Right there, nestled among the sheep and the suspicion of inbreeding, lies Plumpton Place —

a moated Elizabethan manor that looks like it should come with a National Trust tea room but instead was once owned by Jimmy Page himself. That's right, guitar god, black magic enthusiast, and man who probably hasn't washed a dish since 1973. He turned the place into his own personal riff-riddled fortress of solitude, complete with a home studio where parts of *In Through the Out Door* were cooked up — because what better way to shred solos than surrounded by centuries-old beams and the faint smell of medieval mildew?

And the house? Oh, it's the stuff of fantasy. Moat. Tudor windows. The kind of kitchen where you just know someone once salted a pig. Page even appears there in *The Song Remains the Same*, playing a hurdy-gurdy by a misty lake like a druid who got into prog rock. You've not lived until you've watched a man in wizard sleeves summon the gods of rock beside a duck pond.

A hurdy-gurdy, by the way, in case you've somehow lived this long without encountering one (lucky you), is basically what happens when a violin and a medieval crankshaft have an awkward one-night stand and raise the offspring on folk festivals and body odour. It's a stringed instrument you play by turning a handle while pressing keys, making noises that sound like a drunk bagpipe trying to flirt with a lawnmower. Popular in ye olde times when people didn't have Spotify and had to *suffer*.

Anyway, there I was, biking past what looked like the set of *Downton Abbey Does LSD*, knowing that behind those grand old walls, Zeppelin once cranked amps to eleven while I struggled to find a bin for my banana peel.

And me? I was pedalling on like the village idiot who missed the golden age of rock and somehow ended up in lycra, rolling toward Eastbourne with sore thighs and dreams of glory, and at the bottom of my heart, wondering why I had even started this torture of a bike ride.

Just after Plumpton, the path decided it was bored of going gently east and instead took a dramatic, unannounced right turn and headed due south — like it had suddenly remembered it had a hair appointment in Brighton. For a while it played nice, ambling along a pleasant little plateau, giving me the illusion that life was good and gravity had finally called it a day.

But no. This was merely the warm-up. Because not long after, the trail morphed into what I can only describe as a *vertical chalk slide for suicidal cyclists*. The sort of descent that makes you briefly consider writing a will mid-ride. It started steep... and then got *steeper*, like the ground was actively trying to eject me from Sussex.

My speed built up fast. Very fast. Ludicrously fast. But the path was empty, and time was slipping away, so I thought, *sod it* — let's ride this chaos comet. I tucked in, embraced the madness, and began racking up the miles like a lycra-clad Evel Knievel on a sugar high. I covered a couple of miles in what felt like thirty-seven seconds, wind howling, eyes watering, adrenaline pumping in places I didn't even know I had.

And there it was below me—*the main road*. My next death trap. I was now bombing downhill at a speed that would make Top Gear presenters weep with joy, with nothing between me and the tarmac except a fence, a chalk path, and my sense of impending doom.

Time to brake.

Newsflash: the brakes had *opinions*. And those opinions were "No." My pads, worn down to the moral equivalent of a broken promise after days of enthusiastic hill-humping, were now about as effective as a stern look. I pulled harder. *Still nothing*. Pulled tighter. *Slight deceleration*. Not enough. I was now flailing at my handlebars like I was trying to summon divine intervention via aggressive squeezing.

And then — *SNAP*. My back brake cable gave up on life entirely, probably with a little sigh of "I've done all I can." Suddenly I was flying downhill with only one functioning brake and the stopping power of a motivational quote.

So, I did what any rational adult would do: I used my *feet*.

Yes. I scraped them along the chalk path like some deranged Fred Flintstone, desperately trying to create friction with sheer panic and hiking boots. My shoes screamed. My legs screamed. *I screamed.* I came to a stop just inches — *INCHES!* — from the fence, heart pounding, legs jelly, dignity somewhere near Worthing.

Honestly, someone should've handed me a Mission: Impossible theme tune and a slow clap. I deserved at least a BAFTA. Possibly a knighthood. Or, at minimum, a new pair of socks.

As the dust (and bits of my shoe sole) settled, I looked up to find two pensioners seated neatly under a tree, perched in their little camping chairs like extras from a National Trust picnic scene — mouths agape, sandwiches hovering mid-air, completely frozen. Clearly, I'd just interrupted their ham and pickle with a live-action performance of *Cyclist Nearly Dies: The Musical*. I gave them a winning grin and, without missing a beat, said, "And *that*, ladies and gents, is why you don't skip leg day." Then I popped through the gate like it was a stage exit, feeling absolutely majestic. Finally — *finally* — someone had witnessed my greatness. I was a chalk-streaked legend on wheels.

It's a shame I then immediately tripped over

my own bike and went face-first into the path like a majestic idiot swan-diving into disgrace. One moment I was a high-speed, chalk-dusted hero — next, I was face-down in the dirt, legs tangled in the frame like a sad modern art installation titled *"Regret in Lycra."* I could actually *hear* the pensioners' sandwiches being slowly lowered in disbelief.

After dusting myself off — physically, emotionally, and spiritually — I checked the bike for damage. The back brake was still very much dead, and fixing it on the trail would've required either A) a qualified welder or B) a new brake cable and the will to live, neither of which were currently in my possession. So I did the next best thing: tightened the front brake until it sort of hissed in protest, patted the handlebars like "there, there," and carried on like the complete liability that I was.

The path took me over a main road — a dual carriageway, no less — because clearly I hadn't played enough games of *Crossy Road* for one lifetime. I sprinted across like a heavily-armoured frog with commitment issues and emerged victorious on the other side, and then realised there was a bridge just a short distance away. A bridge. A bloody bridge.

Next was a hill charmingly named Loose Bottom. Which, if we're being brutally honest, was also a fairly accurate description of my current physical state. My glutes had more or less given up, and everything below the waist was being held together by hope and flapjack crumbs.

And then, because of *course* it wasn't over, the path immediately went uphill. Again. Really? Was this a trail or some kind of endurance-based punishment for sins I don't remember committing? I slogged up what I assumed was Kingston Hill, though frankly by this point it could've been Mount Doom and I wouldn't have questioned it.

I gave it everything I had on the climb. Truly. I stood on the pedals, leaned into the incline, gritted my teeth like some tragic Lycra-clad war hero, and told myself I *would* conquer this hill. For a moment, I really believed it. I imagined planting a little flag at the top, maybe saluting dramatically while a brass band played in the distance.

But then my legs tapped out, my lungs filed a formal complaint, and my willpower quietly slipped out the back door. It was either get off and push or die dramatically in a chalky heap, and while the latter would've made a good chapter ending, it felt a bit premature. The trail had won this battle. Fine. But I would win the war. Eventually. Probably. Assuming no more brake-related disasters.

So I dismounted with as much grace as a

man who's lost all feeling in his lower half can muster, and I pushed. Boldly. Begrudgingly. Uphill, onward, upward — like a reluctant, slightly sweaty explorer discovering the outer limits of his own endurance. To my left, towns began to peek into view, clustered in the valley below like little promises of future snacks, toilets, and paved surfaces. Civilization! A reminder that one day, somehow, this would end. Probably with chips.

The first one? Kingston! No, not that one. Or that one. Or the other twelve. This is Kingston *near Lewes*, because apparently naming places sensibly was too much to ask from history. Without the "near Lewes" bit, you'd probably end up lost in Surrey, or maybe Jamaica, or worse, *Kingston upon Thames*, elbowing your way through artisan sourdough and people who say "literally" too much. So yes — *this* Kingston had to tack on its geographical cling-on just to be noticed. Bless.

Tucked into the South Downs like it's hiding from something, Kingston near Lewes is one of those places that looks straight out of a countryside brochure—flint cottages, rolling fields, the occasional deer that looks like it pays council tax. It's quaint in that dangerously smug way, like it knows it could be on an overpriced jigsaw puzzle.

The local pub is called The Juggs, which — don't worry — has *nothing* to do with what you just thought. (You filthy animal.) It's named after the big baskets used by fishwives from Brighton who'd hike over the hills to peddle mackerel to the people of Lewes. Because what could pair better with your pint than the mental image of a 19th-century woman hauling 30 pounds of cod in a wicker boob metaphor?

The next village was Swanborough, which I didn't so much cycle through as glide silently above — like a sweaty, lycra-clad drone of judgment. From my lofty perch on the hill, it looked perfectly pleasant, in that unremarkable "could be a retirement ad, could be a hostage situation" kind of way. Apparently, nothing has *ever* happened there. No famous residents, no juicy scandals, not even a modestly rebellious parish council dispute. It's the village equivalent of beige wallpaper — polite, inoffensive, and instantly forgettable. Swanborough: proudly doing absolutely nothing since forever.

Then came Iford — not to be confused with Ilford, which at least has the decency to be grim enough for people to have heard of it. Iford is like Kingston's awkward cousin: same old flint cottages, same sleepy vibe, but with a name that just screams "post code mix-up waiting to happen." While Ilford has a tube station, traffic, and an overwhelming sense of existential dread, *Iford* has... sheep. That's it. Sheep and the low hum of people desperately pretending to enjoy country walks.

Next up: Rodmell, and finally — *finally* — a village with actual historical credentials that don't involve livestock or confusing signage. Rodmell was once home to Virginia Woolf, literary genius, modernist icon, and woman who could write a sentence longer than most of my relationships.

Now, for the philistines among you who think Virginia Woolf is maybe a type of expensive yarn or a discontinued biscuit — no. She was a writer. A very famous, very clever, very complicated writer. Think stream-of-consciousness novels, feminism, emotional turmoil, and parties that involved aggressively intellectual small talk and probably not enough cheese.

She wrote *To the Lighthouse*, *Mrs Dalloway*, and *Orlando*, which involved time travel, gender-swapping, and absolutely zero explanation, because that's what you can get away with when you're a genius with a quill and a nervous disposition. She was part of the Bloomsbury Group, a collection of bohemian intellectuals who all shagged each other and wrote furiously about it afterward.

Rodmell is where she lived, walked, thought big thoughts, and eventually drowned herself in the River Ouse, because sadly, mental health in the early 20th century was mostly treated with strong tea and uncomfortable silences.

At the bottom of the hill lay Southease, which I very delicately *eased* myself into using the one remaining brake I hadn't yet destroyed. I'd been worried that, having tightened it within an inch of its squeaky little life, it might suddenly grab too hard and catapult me over the handlebars like a budget stuntman in a tragic remake of *E.T.*. But no such drama. Turns out, the brake was *not* that good, had *never* been that good, and was now operating purely on optimism and worn rubber. Stopping was more of a suggestion than a function.

To add to the fun, my bike seat had chosen this particular descent to loosen itself and begin tilting forwards like it was trying to eject me through the handlebars *without* involving the brake. Every bump encouraged a more aggressive pelvic nosedive, until I was essentially riding in a yoga position called *Downward Regret*.

Desperate, I ransacked my pannier bags like a man searching for a winning lottery ticket in a bin. Finally, deep in the sweaty abyss of cable ties and old flapjack, I found it — the sacred *Allen key*. The right size! A rare miracle! I shoved it triumphantly into place and tightened like my life depended on it. Which, to be fair, it kind of did.

Nothing.

Tighter. Still nothing.

The thread was gone. Stripped. Dead. My seat was now just a decorative suggestion. A soft, treacherous slide into spinal realignment. Brilliant.

As for Southease, it is the kind of village that looks like it was designed by someone who thought "quaint" was a competitive sport. Thatched cottages? Check. Village green? Naturally. A church with a round tower? Of course — because why settle for the ordinary when you can have a medieval architectural quirk? St. Peter's Church boasts one of only three round towers in Sussex, all nestled in the Ouse Valley. It's like the village got a memo saying, "Be adorable," and took it very seriously.

As I pedalled through this postcard-perfect scene, I crossed the River Ouse — a name so overused in England it's practically the John Smith of rivers. There are at least five River Ouses in the country, which seems less like a coincidence and more like a deliberate attempt by charming villages to confuse outsiders. "Oh, you're looking for the Ouse? Which one?" It's the geographical equivalent of a wink and a nudge.

But Southease isn't just about aesthetic appeal and playful nomenclature. It's also the final resting place of Virginia Woolf, the literary powerhouse known for works like *Mrs Dalloway* and *To the Lighthouse*. In March 1941, after battling mental health issues exacerbated by the war, she filled her pockets with stones and walked into the River Ouse near her home in Rodmell. Her body was discovered weeks later near Southease.

So, as you glide through Southease, take a moment to appreciate its serene beauty, its subtly mischievous place names, and its unexpected brush with literary history. Because just around the corner, in the neighbouring village of Rodmell, is Monk's House — Virginia Woolf's home, sanctuary, and final resting place. Her ashes are buried in the garden beneath two intertwined elm trees, which is poetic, tragic, and also slightly goth in the best possible way.

And where exactly is Monk's House? Oh, it's on a street charmingly — *and confusingly* — named The St. Whether that stands for *The Street* or *The Saint*, I never found out. I'd like to think it's deliberately vague, in keeping with the entire region's campaign to make navigation feel like solving a cryptic crossword on a unicycle. But hey — if you're going to get lost, you might as well do it somewhere this pretty.

The clock was ticking, the shadows were getting longer, and the sun had officially entered its *"I'm out of here, good luck with the hills"* phase of the day. It was time to move on — mainly because if I sat still any longer, I risked fusing permanently with my saddle. Off I went, creaking into motion like a pensioner at a yoga retreat.

And of course, the trail immediately got ugly. Not emotionally. *Topographically.* The path turned uphill again — because apparently, Satan personally designed this final section. Welcome to Beddingham Hill, which sounds gentle but climbs like it's trying to punish you for your life choices. My legs, now operating on sheer caffeine and petty vengeance, screamed the entire way up. The good news? I could see everything. The bad news? I could see *everything* — meaning I could also see how bloody far there still was to go. But the views, to be fair, were stupidly beautiful. Northward: endless Wealdy glory. Southward: the sea, glistening like it was taunting me with the promise of chips and collapse.

Then came the glorious high point — literally — Firle Beacon. I stopped, mostly because my thighs were threatening to go on strike, but also because this spot deserved a moment. Not just for the views, which were offensively spectacular, but for the absolutely bonkers legend it's sitting on.

So here's the tale: Firle Beacon was once home to a giant. Yes, a *giant*. I mean, nothing says "historical accuracy" like a bloke the size of a lighthouse lobbing rocks for fun. Apparently, he got into a turf war with another giant over on Wilmington Hill (because giants are famously territorial and bad at conflict resolution). They had a good old-fashioned stone-throwing battle — like cavemen with terrible aim — and the Firle giant won. How do we know? Because the loser is allegedly buried face-up on Wilmington Hill and now immortalised as the Long Man of Wilmington, a giant chalk figure carved into the hillside. Essentially a prehistoric billboard for "don't mess with Firle."

As for Firle's own giant figure? Gone. Worn away. *Ghosted by erosion.* It was called "Firle Corn" for reasons that are unclear but probably had something to do with ancient fertility cults, phallic symbolism, or some Druid getting wildly carried away with a bit of chalk and a hangover.

But there's more, as Firle Beacon is not only a scenic Sussex high point with breathtaking views and a rich history, but, according to locals in the 1960s, it was also the unlikely site of a bloody *alien invasion*. Yes, move over Roswell, because apparently the South Downs had their very own intergalactic incident — complete with flashing lights, mysterious shapes, and probably at least one bloke screaming "WE'RE ALL GONNA DIE" into his pint.

It all started with strange lights in the sky — the classic "hovering orb of doom" nonsense. Naturally, this was long before drones, lasers, or common sense, so people leapt to the most obvious conclusion: *aliens*. Extraterrestrials.

Visitors from the stars. Who, for reasons no one can quite explain, had bypassed New York, Paris, and Tokyo to beam themselves into a cow field near Lewes.

Eyewitness accounts varied wildly — some saw a glowing saucer, others a "cigar-shaped craft," and at least one woman described it as "a spinning light that made my dog cry." Which, in fairness, also describes most garden security lights.

Soon, word spread, and Firle was transformed into Britain's least glamorous Area 51. Amateur investigators swarmed the hill, armed with binoculars, notepads, and the unwavering belief that aliens had a particular fondness for the A27 corridor. There were reports of scorched grass, strange noises, and one man who swore blind he'd "felt a presence," although that presence later turned out to be indigestion from a dodgy pasty.

Was it a weather balloon — a military test — Barry from Brighton with a torch and a vivid imagination? We'll never know. But for one glorious, slightly drunken summer, Sussex was on high alert for an alien invasion so underwhelming it didn't even make the BBC.

And let's be honest — if intelligent life really *did* visit Firle Beacon, they probably hovered for a bit, observed humanity failing to assemble a deck chair in the wind, and quietly left without saying anything. Which, frankly, is the most relatable thing they've ever done.

So there I stood, surrounded by legends of bickering giants and invisible ancient body art and possibly aliens, with the wind in my face and a suspicious clicking sound coming from somewhere in the bike's undercarriage. I was battered, I was broken, and I was still bloody miles from Eastbourne — but I was on top of the world, baby. And downhill was coming. Maybe. Please. For the love of thighs — *please*.

Thankfully — *miraculously* — the path did finally decide to descend. And thank God, because I was knackered. I'd been going uphill so long I was beginning to worry I'd accidentally entered orbit. Unfortunately, while gravity was now my best mate, my *brakes* were most definitely not. Between the back one that had given up the will to live three hills ago and the front one that now squealed in protest like a hamster with gout, I wasn't exactly filled with confidence.

So down I went. Fast. Faster. *Too* fast. I wasn't so much cycling as free-falling on wheels, praying I didn't end up as a chalky smear on some walker's Instagram story. But somehow, through a combination of sheer luck, shoe-drag braking, and panic-induced posture control, I made it all the way down to Alfriston without dying. Which was nice.

There, I was presented with a choice. A fork in

the literal and metaphorical road. Option A: Stay inland and visit the Long Man of Wilmington, Sussex's giant hillside doodle of questionable anatomical accuracy. Option B: Head south toward Beachy Head, the dramatic chalk cliff known mostly for *that* kind of reputation — the sort that has you questioning your life choices even if you just came for the view. Don't worry, I wasn't considering any drastic action — I just thought *if* I were to keel over, it'd be a pretty spot to do it. Plus, I was curious. And tired. So very, *very* tired.

I needed guidance. Divine intervention. A sign from the cosmos.

Naturally, I used the scientific method: a coin toss.

I pulled a battered 50p from the depths of my pocket and declared, "Heads: the Long Man. Tails: Beachy Head." I tossed it high into the air, and for a brief, glorious moment, time slowed down. The coin flipped, glinting in the golden light, spinning like a scene from a dramatic BBC drama with a slightly too emotional soundtrack.

And then... it landed. Not on heads. Not on tails.

On its bloody edge.

I blinked. Stared. Prodded it with a suspicious finger. No, seriously — *on its edge*. Like some kind of supernatural vending machine glitch. I hadn't seen this happen since I was ten, and even then I assumed it was wizardry or static cling. The ground wasn't even flat! It was chalk and gravel and goat tracks! What were the odds? (Mathematically? Something like 1 in 6,000. Emotionally? Absolute bollocks.)

Then, just as I was about to question reality entirely, the coin *moved*. Just a whisper of a wobble. Then a little more. It teetered. Tilted. And then, slowly, gently, with all the dramatic flair of a Shakespearean death scene... fell to tails.

Beachy Head it was.

Decision made by the will of fate, physics, and sheer sass, I remounted my half-functioning bicycle... and immediately realised I needed the loo. Because after all that cosmic drama and near-death descending, my bladder had decided it was no longer in the business of being ignored.

Beachy Head could wait. *Needs must.*

I soon spotted The Star Inn, and for a brief, responsible second, considered locking up my bike. Then I actually *looked* at my bike. With its squeaky chain, misaligned everything, and the general vibe of "stolen from a skip and immediately regretted," it was clear no one in their right mind would want it. If anything, I should've put a sign on it that said *"Free to emotionally unstable home."*

Inside, I made a tactical dash to the loo — *sorry*

to whoever came in after me. I don't know what you were expecting, but if it wasn't a post-hill, half-dehydrated cyclist apocalypse, then that's on you. I emerged lighter, slightly ashamed, and in urgent need of both sustenance and self-respect.

Time was ticking. Eastbourne still existed. I wasn't there yet. But... it was summer. The light was lingering. And quite frankly, I deserved something fried. So I chucked the day's schedule in the metaphorical bin and ordered the holy trinity of pub survival: fish, chips, and a celebratory pint of ale. Was I technically finished? No. Was I behaving like someone who gave a toss? Also no. And in my defence, I was in and out in under an hour, which in pub terms is basically a tactical military strike.

Now, let's talk about The Star Inn itself — because this place is not just a pub, it's a *medieval fever dream*. Built in 1345 (yes, that's *13-freaking-45*), it started life as a religious hostel, where monks from Battle Abbey put up weary pilgrims on their way to Chichester Cathedral. Back then it was all sandals, sin, and a lot of snoring.

Come the 1500s, the place ditched the god squad and became a fully-fledged public house — basically the spiritual evolution from "holy retreat" to "let's have six pints and tell Steve we love him." And here's a treat: inside the bar still stands a Sanctuary Post, which, in ye olden times, was a bit like tagging base in a drunken game of murder hide-and-seek. Touch the post = safe from arrest. Ideal for anyone who accidentally stole a horse or said something rude about the king's tights.

Oh, and the red lion figurehead outside? Allegedly pinched from a Dutch warship that sank in the Channel and dragged back by smugglers at Cuckmere Haven. Because nothing says "village charm" like wreckage theft and mild maritime looting.

So yes, I left Alfriston slightly buzzed, mildly smug, and full of fried carbs.

Though there is one legend I would like to mention before we leave the place behind completely. Alfriston, it turns out, is a place where history, legend, and complete nonsense have been thrown into a barrel, rolled down a hill, and declared "definitely true, probably." Because once upon a time — according to no credible historian ever — the village vicar wasn't just saving souls, he was smuggling spirits. And not the ghostly kind.

Yes, Reverend Sneakyboots (name changed for dramatic effect) is said to have preached fire and brimstone on Sunday morning, then spent Sunday evening elbow-deep in a crate of contraband claret, shouting "Hallelujah!" every time he found an unopened bottle. Apparently, Jesus turned water into wine, and this lad took the hint and opened a full-blown illicit distribution centre beneath the nave.

His church was supposedly riddled with tunnels — after all, nothing screams "place of worship" like a subterranean escape route and a side hustle in Dutch gin. Parishioners would gather for communion while, just metres below, French brandy was being dragged through the crypt like some kind of ecclesiastical Wetherspoons.

And how did he get away with it? Easy. Who's going to suspect the vicar? He's wearing robes, for God's sake. Smugglers don't wear robes! (*Spoiler: they absolutely would if it meant free booze.*)

Of course, there's no real evidence any of this happened. Not a jot. But between you, me and the ghost of Reverend Boozy McBoozeface, it's such a gloriously ridiculous idea that I refuse to let facts ruin it. So next time you pass through Alfriston, give the church a nod, check the floorboards for trapdoors, and remember: sometimes, the path to salvation involves a very large bottle of rum and a clergyman with a criminal record and a drinking problem.

Moving on, the sun dipped low behind me as I pedalled off into the golden haze, like a slightly bloated knight riding off after a round at Ye Olde Wetherspoons. And I still had no back brake. But who needs one when you've got history, ale, and delusion on your side?

After my triumphant pub exit and a brief moment of reflection (read: belching fried cod into the breeze), I hopped back onto my *rusty* — sorry, *trusty* — steed, which at this point creaked more than a haunted wardrobe and handled like a shopping trolley with a limp. But thankfully, the trail decided to give me a break and turned *pleasantly flat* alongside the Cuckmere River. It was a rare and beautiful moment: no uphill suffering, no mechanical failures, just me, some gently babbling water, and the distant sound of my remaining brake whispering "soon..."

I rolled lazily through Litlington, crossed the river, and then — *bam!* — there it was: the Litlington White Horse, plastered boldly across the hillside like a chalky, prehistoric billboard for equestrian enthusiasm. And for a moment, I was genuinely impressed. It's 93 feet long, 65 feet high, and confidently showing its side profile like it's posing for a Renaissance oil painting.

Now, the origins of this magnificent beast are *deeply historical...* allegedly. One tale says it was carved in 1838 to celebrate Queen Victoria's coronation — a patriotic tribute, a symbol of regal strength, a moment of national unity carved into the land itself. God save the Queen and all that.

...Or, and bear with me here, it was actually the result of two bored local lads in the 1860s who saw a patch of exposed chalk and thought, "That kinda looks like a horse's head — shall we do the rest?" And then just *did it*. Because what else is there to do in Litlington when you're a teenage boy in 1860? No Xbox, no Wi-Fi, and a pub that probably served gin in teacups.

The current horsey outline was re-cut in 1924 by three men — John Ade, Mr. Bovis, and Eric Hobbis — who allegedly did the whole thing in a *single night under a full moon*, which is adorable, but let's be honest — there was absolutely beer involved. Probably a lot of it. Possibly absinthe. Who looks at a hillside and thinks, "You know what would look great here? A giant horse we can only see properly from half a mile away"? Men with flasks and no adult supervision, that's who.

Now, during WWII, the horse was *camouflaged*. Yes, camouflaged. Because the British government feared that German bombers might look down from 30,000 feet, spot this majestic chalk equine, and say, "Aha! That's where the entire British military must be hiding!" So they *covered it up*. With turf. Which is like putting a lampshade on your head and calling it stealth mode.

And the horse hasn't had it easy since. It's been neglected, redrawn, faded, defaced, and — in 2017 — someone added a unicorn horn to it. Which, honestly, was probably an improvement. But no, that got removed, presumably by the National

Trust Fun Police.

Still, it's there. Bold. Proud. Chalky. Reminding everyone who passes that Sussex is a place where royalty might be celebrated in grand symbols — or where teenagers just make giant white animals on hillsides for a laugh.

Either way, I loved it. It was the kind of surreal nonsense that makes this country wonderful: pointless, ancient, possibly drunk, and completely unforgettable.

South I went, rolling through blessedly flat terrain like some sort of lycra-clad pilgrim of the coast. The path was kind, the air was soft, and my legs — while still questioning all life choices — had stopped actively plotting my murder. It was almost pleasant. Suspiciously so. And then, as if summoned by a dramatic sound effect, I entered... Friston Forest.

Now, Friston is a lovely place — *if* your idea of lovely is being suddenly surrounded by more dogs than Crufts and enough fleeces to clothe a small nation. The trail was positively *heaving* with dog walkers. Thankfully, the dogs were on leads. The humans, less so. At one point I nearly crashed into a man who'd taken root mid-path while his Labrador attempted to drag a tree into another dimension. Honestly, I don't blame the dogs. If I had four legs and boundless energy, I'd be chasing squirrels too. Instead, I had a wobbly bike and the bladder capacity of a pensioner. Life's not fair.

Onward I rolled into Westdean, which was as peaceful and charming as a postcard on Valium. Lovely little church, neatly arranged houses, and not a single person yelling into a mobile phone. It felt suspiciously wholesome. Then came Exceat (pronounced "Ex-seat," because of course it is) — home to the Seven Sisters Visitor Centre, which was, of course, *closed*. Because I was now entering that magical twilight time known as "past opening hours," when all facilities vanish and you're left alone with your thoughts and a slowly disintegrating protein bar.

We should pause just for a minute at Exceat. Once a thriving Saxon fishing village with views to die for (and oh boy, *they did*), it even got a royal visit in 1305 from Edward I, who probably stopped by just to judge the locals and fart in their direction.

Then along came the Black Death, kicking down doors and wiping out the population like it was collecting loyalty points for the apocalypse. Half the village dropped dead, the other half presumably panicked and invented social distancing 600 years early.

But wait — *plot twist*! Just when things couldn't get worse, the bloody French showed up, doing what the French did best: setting fire to things that weren't theirs and looking smug about it. By

1460, Exceat had more ghosts than people. Two parishioners remained. *Two.* That's not a village, that's not even a pub quiz team.

Then in 1913, a 15-year-old local lad called Maurice Lawrance wandered into a field and casually *discovered the lost church*. Total legend. But because fate is a vindictive twat, Maurice was promptly killed in World War I, proving once again that this village can't have *nice things*.

Today, Exceat is mostly a car park with historical baggage. But if you listen closely, you can still hear the echoes of plague, fire, and teenage archaeological brilliance — assuming the dog walkers haven't drowned it out. There's nothing here, but it's still better than Ilford.

Despite being technically closed, the place was still swarming with people milling about like confused extras in a National Trust promotional video. I made the executive decision to bypass the lot of them, mostly to avoid answering questions like, "Are you doing a sponsored ride?" (No. Just personally sponsored by bad planning and bad knees.)

Out of the forest I came, legs still moving, spirit slightly revived, and then — *bam* — there it was. The sea. The glorious, shimmering, smug English Channel. Just east of Cuckmere Haven, where the river does that scenic wriggly thing you always see on tea towels and Sunday night BBC dramas.

I'd made it. Almost. Not quite Eastbourne yet, but nearly. The coast was within reach. My tyres were still inflated (somehow), my brakes still a rumour, and I was practically vibrating with fried food and defiance.

I was *nearly there*.

And I could see them — the Seven Sisters — Sussex's iconic white chalk cliffs, strutting dramatically along the coast like nature's own runway models. They're the ultimate coastal show-offs: stark, stunning, a bit unstable, and prone to crumbling under pressure — basically the Kardashians of geology.

These chalky queens have been forming for millions of years, built from the compressed remains of tiny sea creatures that died, sank, and said, *"You know what? Let's make a cliff out of this."* Fast forward to now, and voilà — majestic headlands stretching between Seaford and Eastbourne, drawing in hikers, day-trippers, and people with a death wish for a selfie too close to the edge.

And don't let their elegant curves fool you — they're literally falling to pieces. Eroding at about half a metre a year, these ladies are in permanent freefall. So if you want a photo, better get it quick before one of them throws herself dramatically into the Channel like a chalky Kate Winslet.

Of course, they've also had their moment in the spotlight — starring in films and TV shows that need *just the right amount of scenic trauma*. Most famously, they posed as the White Cliffs of Dover in *Robin Hood: Prince of Thieves* — you know, the one where Robin of Loxley somehow travels from Dover to Sherwood Forest via *Hadrian's bloody Wall*. Geography? Never heard of it, apparently.

This was *definitely* not the best spot to admire the Sisters — unless your idea of a panoramic view involves a half-obscured chalky wiggle in the distance while you stand next to a bin and pretend you're having a profound connection with the Earth. I stared at it for a moment, just long enough to say I'd "taken it in," then decided I wasn't about to have my spiritual awakening in what felt like the overflow car park of a lesser nature documentary.

So, off I went, the sun now absolutely flirting with the idea of setting behind me, casting those golden-hour shadows that Instagram influencers pretend just "happen naturally." As I pedalled on, the trail got noticeably busier. After days of solitary smugness, breezing past the occasional walker like some kind of Lycra-clad ghost, I was suddenly surrounded by people. Actual humans. Dozens of them. All clogging up the path with their dogs, their unpredictable children, and their utter refusal to keep to one side.

Apparently, Birling Gap was the place to be — supposedly *the* spot for peak Sister appreciation. Well, it had better be, because if I was going to risk a head-on collision with an unsupervised Labrador, I expected to be moved to tears by the view. Or at the very least, mildly impressed.

I kept pedalling, even though "progress" was perhaps too strong a word for whatever I was doing. The scenery was like a screensaver (ironically, I later discovered that these actual cliffs featured as exactly that way back in the dark days of Windows 7). They were seemingly not changing at all, and the far-off cliffs weren't getting any closer. I was starting to suspect that the whole coastline was just one big geological copy-paste job. Honestly, if you've seen one white cliff, you've pretty much seen them all. Majestic, yes, but after an hour of squinting at yet another sheer chalk drop, even *majestic* starts to feel a bit samey.

And then — just as I was about to stage a personal protest against cliffs and the concept of distance — I was saved by distraction. A memorial. Something new. A shiny slab of history to break up the monotony. I stopped, did the polite thing, dismounted, and thought I'd skim it for the usual local hero backstory. But this one? This one actually delivered.

Ladies and gentlemen, let me introduce you to Captain William Charles Campbell: a man so heroic he made Indiana Jones look like a slightly brave geography teacher.

Born in 1889 in Bordeaux (apparently, being a war hero wasn't *continental* enough) Campbell eventually decided to become one of Britain's most gloriously unhinged flying aces during World War I. He racked up 23 aerial victories, which in modern terms is like getting a platinum trophy in "World War I: Dogfight Edition" on Expert Mode. But unlike the others who spent their time shooting down enemy planes, Campbell had a thing for balloons. Enemy observation balloons, specifically. And he wasn't just casually popping them — he *specialised* in it. Like, if you had a rogue balloon problem, Campbell was your man. He was the first British pilot to earn the title of "balloon buster ace," which sounds like either a wartime legend or a very niche birthday party clown.

But Campbell didn't just float around in a biplane popping balloons. No, this guy would *dive* at them, guns blazing, while dodging heavy ground fire and other planes, and then skim back to base so low he probably had to duck under washing lines. In one of his more ridiculous exploits, he attacked a balloon, set it on fire, came back at *twenty feet* from the ground — twenty! — under heavy fire, just to make sure the job was done. You know how they tell pilots to maintain altitude for safety? Yeah, Campbell heard that and said, "Nah, I'm good."

He got the Distinguished Service Order and a Military Cross with Bar, which is basically the Olympic gold medal triple-crown of military bling — rare, wildly impressive, and just the right amount of "look at me, I'm a legend." He even once attacked and scattered a literal column of enemy troops from the air, like some kind of airborne Deliveroo for chaos.

Eventually, he was wounded — probably by the laws of probability finally catching up with him — and was dragged back to England where someone clearly said, "Right, that's enough near-death for now," and made him Chief Instructor at the School of Military Aeronautics. You know, so he could train other pilots how to fight the war without accidentally inventing base-jumping.

After the war, he gracefully returned to civilian life. And what else do you do after personally punching holes in the sky for your country? Obviously, you become the chairman of Brighton & Hove Albion Football Club. Because why not? It's the natural career progression for a man who once declared war on hydrogen.

So yes, I stopped to read a plaque. And I came away with the story of a man who turned dogfights and balloon busting into an extreme sport. Captain Campbell, you magnificent madman — thank you for making me forget, however briefly, that I was still going absolutely nowhere.

Eventually — after what felt like forty years of pedalling past identical cliffs while being slowly roasted like a Tesco rotisserie chicken — I reached Birling Gap. One minute I was moaning that I'd never get there, and the next — BOOM — there it was, like a chalky mirage. I stopped for the obligatory photo, the kind that says, *Look! I'm appreciating nature and not just dead inside!*, then pushed on towards the legendary, the iconic, the notoriously vertical: Beachy Head.

Ah, Beachy Head. The crown jewel of Britain's "exit strategies." If cliffs could talk, this one would probably say, *"Another one? Bloody hell, take a number."* Because yes, this dramatic hunk of coastline isn't just famous for its sweeping views and howling winds — it's also the third most popular suicide spot in the world. Bronze medal in the global death Olympics, right behind San Francisco's Golden Gate Bridge and Japan's Aokigahara Forest, a.k.a. "The Hanging Gardens of Nope."

The authorities, in a noble but probably exhausting effort, have tried everything to stop people from flinging themselves off the edge. There are signs asking people to "Please consider your family," which is cute, because if you're already up there, odds are you've already considered them and decided they can sod off.

There's also the Beachy Head Chaplaincy Team who patrol the area daily, presumably alternating between heartfelt interventions and wondering why they didn't choose quieter careers like lion-taming or bomb disposal.

Some people say it's the isolation. Others blame the endless wind and the crushing weight of modern life. Me? I think it's because after you've spent two hours trying to park anywhere near the visitor centre and paid £7.80 for a tepid sausage roll, flinging yourself off the cliff starts to look like a perfectly rational form of protest.

Still, despite its morbid reputation, the place is *weirdly* cheery in person. Bright skies, flocks of cheeping tourists, National Trust signs trying really hard to look helpful and not wildly out of their depth. It's like Disneyland, if Disneyland was run by the Grim Reaper and sponsored by Prozac.

I paused for a second, letting the wind smack me in the face like an overexcited aunt who's had one too many sherries at a wedding. This was it. Peak England. Stunning, theatrical, and just the right side of completely unhinged. And then, right on cue, it happened — a seagull took one look at my vibe and shat on me. Because of course it did.

The final stretch still clung to the cliffs, winding its way above the sea like some dramatic closing scene from one of those flagship BBC dramas — except with more leg cramp and fewer brooding orchestral swells. The sun, now basically clocking off for the day, had almost ducked below the horizon behind me, leaving that creeping darkness in its place. Not the gentle, twinkly kind of dusk you get in rom-coms, but the sort of advancing gloom that feels like it's actively hunting you down. If nightfall were a monster, it would have been right on my tail, licking its chops and muttering, *"Run, little cyclist, run."*

I pushed on, pedalling like I was being chased by a tax inspector. The wind picked up, the shadows deepened, and still I clung to the chalky edge of Britain like a stubborn bit of sandwich crust. And then, just as the last streaks of light gave up entirely and buggered off over the Channel — *there I was*. The end. The grand finale. The majestic terminus of my epic journey.

Aaaaand it was… a car park.

A car park. Near a bus stop. On the corner of *Duke's Drive*. No fanfare. No "Welcome to Eastbourne!" sign. Not even a sad little bench with a plaque saying "Well done, you magnificent idiot." Just a patch of tarmac, a few confused motorists, and the gentle glow of a municipal streetlamp humming like it, too, had lost the will to live.

This was it? After cliffs, chaos, chalk, near-death ascents and historical detours through Britain's madness? I'd made it to the end of a national trail and the powers that be had decided not to bother with an actual ending. It was like watching the final episode of a ten-season TV show and finding out it was just a two-minute PowerPoint presentation followed by a Windows shutdown noise.

No café. No sculpture. No commemorative rock. Just a half-hearted whimper into the night as the path limped to a finish line nobody had remembered to mark. Honestly, I've had more dramatic conclusions to a microwave meal.

Still, I'd done it. All the way from Winchester to here. City to almost-but-not-quite-city. My legs were knackered, my arse was numb, and my reward was a view of someone trying to reverse out of a tight parking bay while a child screamed in the background. Beautiful. Timeless. So very, *very* Eastbourne.

Conclusion

I went into Eastbourne, I mean, I had to. What do you think I did — bed down for the night in the bus stop like some sort of Lycra-clad troll, clutching my energy bars and muttering about gradients to passing teenagers? No, I cycled — nay, *hobbled* — into town because I am, against all evidence to the contrary, a grown adult with basic survival instincts.

The following day, I found the station. I looked for a train. And no, my train wasn't late. That would have been adorable. It was cancelled. Completely. The transport equivalent of the universe just sticking two fingers up and yelling, *"Surprise, idiot!"*

So I stood there, broken in spirit and quadriceps, trying to look dignified while Googling how far it was to *literally anywhere else with functioning trains*. Eventually, I got home. Don't ask me how. I think it involved a rail replacement bus, three forms of internal screaming, and a guy eating a Scotch egg in a way that still haunts me.

Looking back — through the hazy, saddle-sore filter of time — it *was* a hell of a trip. The highlights? The views. The sun when it chose to make an appearance. The kind strangers who gave directions, snacks, and just the right amount of sympathy when I looked like I might cry on their dog. The lowlights? Oh, just the tiny things — horizontal rain, hills designed by sadists, the occasional human speed bump masquerading as a fellow path user, and that one guy who told me to "get off the road" while overtaking in a 2003 Vauxhall Zafira with all the subtlety of a chainsaw in a library.

And the dogs. Glorious, glorious dogs. Always up for a sniff, a wag, and occasionally an attempt to trip me into a ditch. Far better company than some of the humans, frankly. Especially the ones who clearly believed cyclists were a plague sent to ruin their peaceful walk to the garden centre.

But you know what? It all came together. The madness, the magic, the mid-ride existential crises. Like some twisted cosmic jigsaw, it aligned — rain, sun, kindness, blisters — all choreographed by the gods of travel to create the *perfect* journey. Well, nearly perfect. That ending in the car park? Still absolute crap. But you can't have everything.

And me? Oh, I was a picture. Sunburnt in patches, salt-streaked, walking like a cowboy who'd picked the wrong saddle. My foolish belief that this would be "a nice little ride" laughed in my face the whole way. I had grand visions of breezing across the coast, wind in my hair, Instagram-worthy moments every mile. What I got was trench foot, an uneven tan, and an existential crisis somewhere near Shoreham.

The only thing more battered than me was the bike. I was going to chuck it in the tip the moment we got home, like a cursed object you need rid of before it steals your soul. But even the tip wouldn't take it. Too dangerous, apparently. So I wheeled it back into my shed — muddy, creaky, still somehow oozing shame — and I'm glad I did. The seat's still broken, the brake's still broken, and the tyres are shot. A bit like me. But we did it, me and that clunky old beast. We saw the South Downs. We conquered the cliffs. And now?

Well, I'll be soaking in my bath, sipping something that burns, and smiling smugly every time someone says, "Oh, you cycled the South Downs Way? That must've been nice."

Nice?

Mate, it was *biblical*.

Printed in Dunstable, United Kingdom